Pastor **James McConnell**

THE GOOD THE BAD & JESUS CHRIST

I TELL IT ALL!

Foreword by Bob Gass

The Good, The Bad & Jesus Christ

Paperback ISBN: 978-0-9934910-0-9
ebook ISBN: 978-0-9934910-1-6

Published by
Maurice Wylie Media
Bethel Media House
Tobermore
Magherafelt,
Northern Ireland
BT45 5SG (UK)

Publishers' statement: *Throughout this book the love for our God is such that whenever we refer to Him we honour with Capitals. On the other hand, when referring to the devil, we refuse to acknowledge him with any honour to the point of violating grammatical rule and withholding a capital.*

www.MauriceWylieMedia.com

PLACING MINISTRY ONTO PAPER

Create | Brand | Establish

DEDICATION

I would like to dedicate this book to my wife Margaret. When we tied the knot 57 years ago who would have thought that God would have taken us on this journey. Thank you for all your love and patience through both the good and difficult times, of which there have been many! I am litterly blessed to have you in my life and also our two beautiful daughters, Linda and Julie. You have all brought so much joy to my heart.

I would also like to thank the members of Whitewell Metropolitan Tabernacle who are one of the finest congregations in the world. I could never have accomplished as much for the Kingdom of God without the faithful support from you, who have stood by me through thick and thin.

Also overseas, I would like to honour my two dear friends in San Antonio, Texas: John and Dale Estlinbaum, whose friendship has been a great encouragement to me during these last 42 years.

CHAPTERS

ENDORSEMENTS 7

FOREWORD 17

INTRODUCTION 19

1 – **WHISTLING IN THE DARK** 21
My beloved mother...

2 – **MY FIRST ENCOUNTER** 27
Speaking in a new language...
Planting pots...

3 – **TAKING ON A TRADE** 35
Do you have a tree?
Preaching, is it an art?

4 – **NAME IN THE 'BLACK BOOKS'** 41
Measured blessings...
The wrapping must match the gift...
Man in the tea cosy...

5 – **A CROWD OF ONE** 49
The lady with the flowing hair...
The call of God...

6 – **CONTROVERSIAL MENTORS** 55
In a dry land...

7 – **CRIED LIKE A BABY** 61
Washing the dishes...
Unwillingness to surrender...
The first service...

8 – **THE McCONNELLS** 71
The next George Best?
A very special moment...
Confession: good for the soul...

9 – **AN AMAZING TESTIMONY** 79
Thirteen years lost...
Stormy seasons in our lives...
Carpet in, carpet out...

10 – **MAKING PROTESTANTS?** 87
The big man and me...

11 – **MAN IN THE GALLERY** 91
Winning souls...
The man in the mirror...

12 – **MEGA-CHURCH IN THE MAKING** 95
It's time to get right...

13 – **TO THE ENDS OF THE EARTH** 99

14 – **CANCER COMES KNOCKING** 103

15 – **HOPE NO ONE IS WATCHING** 109
The harvest is white...

16 – **ROMANIAN ORPHANAGE** 117
Helping the disadvantaged in Kenya...
Rapid growth in Ethiopia...

17 – **COURTING FAITH** 125
A year later...
Stand up, stand up for Jesus...

18 – **THE RIGHT OF FREE SPEECH** 135
Reflecting on the trial...

19 – **LOVED BY GOD** 143

20 – **WHEN THE HOUSE DIVIDES** 153
My failing health...

21 – **PASSING THE BATON** 161

22 – **TURNING FEAR TO FAITH** 167
A spirit of fear

23 – **THE ROYAL HEM** 173

WHO IS JESUS? 182

ENDORSEMENTS

"Every life from start to finish is a tapestry being woven. Each thread woven into our particular tapestry to form our picture is the influence and impact of various people providence allows to cross our paths. When I was only a few weeks old, God began to weave a 'special thread' into my life. The name of this particular thread was James McConnell. He was my parents' minister and they took me to the Orange Hall where Gospel meetings were being held, for him to give thanks to God for their firstborn and to ask God for His hand to be on my life. Every week, my parents took me to church and over the years James McConnell's ministry began to shape my thinking, as I listened to the gospel he preached, learning of a glorious Saviour and my own personal need of salvation. I was thirteen when, after a sermon the pastor preached, I trusted Christ as my Lord and Saviour."

"Pastor McConnell was more than a minister. He was like family. When my father was murdered by terrorists, he had the unenviable task of breaking the news to me and I still recall how we wept on each other's shoulder that dark January evening. The Divine weaver was weaving this special thread further and further into the tapestry of my life."

"Examine the life of David Purse and the golden thread that is James McConnell, repeatedly appears. He has been my pastor, my friend, my helper, my inspiration, my example and father in the gospel that the Almighty used over and over again to shape and define the picture that is my life. Thank you Pastor for the impact you have had and the influence you have been in my life."

Pastor David Purse
Senior Pastor, Whitewell Tabernacle, Belfast.

*****

"Pastor James McConnell, affectionately known as the Bishop, is a born preacher. His preaching is powerful, convicting, solid, balanced and penetrating in application. I have seen him touch the lives of thousands of people of all ages and social backgrounds."

"His love for Christ and the gospel is unparalleled. He has never lost his passion for lost souls. His love for God's people has never waned. His drive to see the Kingdom of God extended is relentless. The steadfastness of his vision and zeal makes this book a must-read for everyone."

Pastor Michael Bunting
Whitewell Metropolitan Church, Belfast

*****

"I grew up in Pastor McConnell's church, The Whitewell Metropolitan Tabernacle. I came to faith as a seven-year-old through his preaching of God's Word. At age thirty I began full-time ministry as a pastor in Whitewell."

"Pastor McConnell has been one of the greatest evangelists in Ireland in modern times, leading tens of thousands of souls to Christ. Travelling the world and building schools, churches, orphanages and medical centres for disadvantaged children. He has achieved many great things, but not for himself, for the Kingdom of God. I can recount times visiting hospitals with him where patients with dementia became clear of mind to talk of salvation. Times of miracles and healing in the congregation, times of personal sacrifice and suffering because of God's call on his life."

"One thing is sure: it is certain this man has been touched by God and although we all exist within our own humanity, Pastor McConnell has also managed to live and pursue those things that are above. He has been a gift from God to this generation: a watchman, a shepherd and a servant."

Pastor David Murray
Whitewell Metropolitan Church, Belfast

*****

"What can I say about Pastor McConnell? Or the Bishop, as he is affectionately known. I first heard him preach on 31st January 1982, which was the night I was saved for the first time in my life. I heard this man say that he loved Jesus and this had a life-changing impact on me, as it was the vehicle that brought me to trust in the Lord Jesus Christ."

"In 1987 my Mum took ill and I called at the church to ask Pastor McConnell to pray for her, which he said he would. Later I found out that within half an hour of seeing him he had gone to the Moyle hospital in Larne to visit her. He wanted to check that she was okay with Jesus! Unfortunately, my Mum passed away a few days later, but I will never forget his thoughtfulness and concern for his congregation, which meant so much to me."

Pastor Frankie Weir
Whitewell Metropolitan Church, Belfast.

*****

"I have known Pastor James McConnell for over twenty-one years and was saved under his ministry at the Whitewell Metropolitan Tabernacle in Belfast. He is a true servant of God

- an evangelist with a passion for souls, as well as having a caring, pastoral heart. There is no doubt he is a unique, once in a generation leader, who has been an inspiration to many, including me, over the years. He has been a shining light for the cause of the Gospel of the Lord Jesus Christ, not only in his homeland of Northern Ireland, but also right around the world, as God has blessed the faithfulness of the 'Bishop' as he's affectionately known."

"Pastor McConnell's love for the Lord Jesus Christ drives everything that he does, and it means he sets the very best example to those around him. Even in retirement he hasn't quite hung up his preaching boots yet, and I don't believe he ever will as long as there is strength left in his body. That is the heart of the man and long may it continue!"

Pastor Nigel Begley
Whitewell Metropolitan Church, Belfast

*****

"Pastor McConnell or 'the Bishop' as he is affectionately known was 45-years-old when I first encountered him. I was a young man of 24 the first Sunday night I was invited by a friend and neighbour of mine, Frank Weir, to the Whitewell church on June 13th 1984 to hear him preach the Gospel. When Pastor McConnell made the appeal that night for people to get saved, I responded. Since that night he has had a remarkable impact on my life and that of my family who attend the Tabernacle."

"Through his dedication and faithfulness to The Lord Jesus Christ, I have grown to love and respect him as one of a rare breed of servants of God who truly loves The Lord. That is one thing about him that has never changed or faltered no matter what has came his way, both good and not so good."

"The Pastor still preaches The Lord Jesus Christ with the same passion and zeal as he did the very first night I heard him. His influence inspired me to enter the ministry and I have worked alongside him since 1992. His ministry still challenges and inspires young men and women, and the not so young, to serve The Lord all over the world."

Pastor Shaw Higgins
Whitewell Metropolitan Church, Belfast

*****

"As a young lad of fifteen, I was invited to the Orange Hall one Sunday in 1964. I went with my younger brother and what I heard was a hungry pastor who preached from his heart.

"In those days the church was small and if a visitor appeared it was like the song "Some enchanted evening, you will see a stranger." The Lord moved and saved my family one by one. I remember Pastor McConnell who lived in relative poverty back then; when he prayed on his knees you could see the holes in his shoes!"

"However, God honoured His Word and started blessing him with souls and has never stopped since then."

Pastor William McTernaghan
Whitewell Metropolitan Church, Belfast

*****

"At the age of 25, I walked into the old church at Whitewell, in a state of rebellion against God. As I sat under Pastor McConnell I recognised the truth and realised that I had a very big decision to make. I would either embrace the truth or reject it. Pastor McConnell made it very clear that there was no room for fence-selling. After fighting the Lord for weeks, I finally threw the hands up and yielded to Him."

"One thing I always appreciated about Pastor McConnell was, he did not try to dilute the truth, he did not try to explain it away. He always said it the way it was. He called a spade a spade!"

"Whitewell became my spiritual home and personal Bible school. It was there that I learned to love the Lord, and it was there that I learned to dig deep in His Word. Pastor McConnell made Jesus alive. He made the Word of God personal to me. He gave me a hunger for the Scriptures. He also showed me that ministry was a lifestyle."

"Through the direction and correction of the Word, I felt the call of God to be a pastor. Today, the Lord has given me the great honour of being a full-time pastor on the Omaha Indian reservation in Nebraska. Having sat under Pastor McConnell for ten years, I find myself quoting him all the time. He would often say to the young preachers: 'Always preach for a verdict.' That is something I have tried to apply to every message I preach."

Pastor Paul Malcomson
Light of the World Gospel Ministries, Walthill, Nebraska

*****

"It was an amazing night in Whitewell. Pastor McConnell had preached 'a storm' to over 3,000 people and dozens received Jesus. After the service he came down from the platform directly to me, an unknown visitor in his church and said; "Son, you need to come and see me!" It was an answer to the prayer of this 35-year-old business man with the call of God on his life, who didn't know what to do with it or how to go about it."

"Our first meeting in the church café was so different from what I had expected. Here was the same man who delivered the awesome, powerful, anointed word from God on Sunday night and yet here was a warm and down-to-earth man who was genuinely concerned for my situation. He didn't have to help at all but his wisdom in leadership proved his ministry to be good. Given my position of responsibility to and for all the families at Wrightbus, his belief was that I should 'prove out' this call of God on my life and if I would give him one day of my week he would train me. That continued for five years."

"Here with this man, this servant, I learned of his love for Jesus and came to understand that loving Jesus is ministry. Without Jesus and His love, there is no ministry. We truly are standing on the shoulders of a giant of the faith and a giant in good ministry. Thank you Pastor."

Pastor Jeff Wright
Green Pastures, Ballymena

*****

"During sixty years of full-time ministry and service in the Kingdom of God, Pastor James McConnell has seen thousands come to saving faith in the Lord Jesus Christ. From the religious to the atheist, the agnostic or the addict, they all come through the anointed, faithful preaching of the precious word of truth. Lives have been changed, given direction and hope. I was one of those souls saved and a life changed, delivered from alcohol and drug addiction."

"Pastor McConnell is a man who loves the Lord Jesus and through the agency of the Holy Spirit and the Word of God he has taught me to love Jesus, to see Him in all the Scriptures and to be devoted to Christ alone. Through James McConnell's ministry I was tutored and given the opportunity to enter full-time ministry to serve the Lord."

"I am grateful to God for James McConnell and I pray for God's continued blessing upon him. Thank you my Pastor for your faithfulness to the preaching of the cross, the blood and the book."

"I thank my God upon every remembrance of you."
Philippians 1:3

Pastor Ken Davidson
Donaghcloney Elim Church

"Pastor James McConnell, a born leader, has been an instrument in the hand of God, as he has explained and proclaimed God's precious Word not only in his beloved Whitewell, but in the many countries he has visited. His rich motivational ministry has made an indelible impression upon the lives of those who have listened to it. His evangelistic zeal and uncompromising commitment to the Word of God has always been at the forefront of everything that he did, nothing was allowed to eclipse the teaching of Scripture, or dilute his gift to preach the Gospel. He always took every opportunity to, in his own words, throw out the net".

"Holy Spirit leadership, born out of an encounter with Almighty God, has marked out the ministry of this ordinary man doing extraordinary things. A man who unashamedly believes in the inerrant and eternal Word of God, and preaches with conviction and compassion as a faithful ambassador of the One who called him and anointed him for the ministry. James believes in the message he preaches, and has never resorted to gimmicks, current fads, or sought to satisfy the whims and fancies of any congregation. Rather, he consciously and continuously proclaims what people need to hear, rather than what they want to hear. Deference and timidity have never been part of his make-up, as he sought to awaken souls, for whom Christ died."

"His life's work which has resulted in outstanding church growth, has also encountered much opposition, ridicule, and many false allegations from the armchair critics. However, undeterred as a 'gospel-driven pastor' he refuses to be bound by compliance to public opinion, or legislation which is to the detriment of the work of God. Rather prayer, hearing from God, and the exposition of God's Word are the hallmarks of Pastor McConnell's ministry, a man whose ministry has been faithfully supported at all times, the good and the bad by his loving wife Margaret."

"We have all only one life to live. Pastor McConnell has lived his, knowing that only what's done for Jesus will last. Well done James and Margaret."

Eric McComb

Superintendent of Elim Churches in Ireland (1979-2011)

“Many years ago, James McConnell heard the call of God to yield his life to the ministry of proclaiming the Gospel of the Lord Jesus Christ, as the only Saviour of men and women from the penalty of sin. He has been faithful to the call of God.”

“His life echoes the words of Paul the Apostle; ‘For to me, to live is Christ.’ God has blessed him in his ‘Christ-centred’ ministry using him to bring a multitude of men and women to a saving knowledge of the Lord Jesus Christ.”

“His expository preaching has been the inspiration of many young men to follow him into ministry for the Lord Jesus.”

To God be the glory!

Eric Briggs, retired Pastor

*****

“In 2015, I came to hear of the case of Pastor James McConnell’s persecution for preaching his doctrinal criticisms of Islamic beliefs - matters about which Jim McConnell and I will, of course, disagree as Christian and Muslim clergymen. I remember vividly my smarting emotional response as I was reading the story of this criminalising of a man of my own father’s age and moral outlook, and dismay; not at Pastor James’s preaching, but rather that in the eight hundredth year of Magna Carta, the state should trespass on spiritual matters of a man’s heart. I couldn’t do anything other than speak up on this ethical issue, and so I picked up the phone and called Pastor Jim.”

“I didn’t know what to expect, and was immediately moved by the gentleness of Pastor Jim’s welcome and kindness to me. That day I met a true Christian who preached hard words in his seeking after truth and simultaneously offered boundless love to me in generous grace and friendship.”

“There are moments in life when God’s Hand is heavy upon

events, and the Court case was such an occasion. I rapidly discovered among Pastor Jim's close friends, Catholic and Protestant, black and white, that while there were times we were desperately worried how the legal process would go, we had no doubt that in the eyes of heaven, Pastor James McConnell had already won!"

"Pastor Jim and our friends continue our commitment to work together for the cause of persecuted Christians and other vulnerable people, and upholding the precious freedom of conscience to disagree in brotherly love - something for which unnumbered innocent people daily lay down their lives."

Sheikh Dr Muhammad Al-Hussaini,
Senior Fellow in Islamic Studies at the Westminster Institute

FOREWORD

Jim McConnell is my friend, and I have always loved him. There are so many reasons. It was listening to him preach as a 19-year-old evangelist, that I was won to Christ and called to the ministry. I was only twelve at the time. And like him, I preached my first sermon one year later at age thirteen. I was mentored in ministry by a brilliant Bible expositor called Dr Gordon Magee and several other wonderful ministers, including Jim. But I noticed something unique about Jim. When he preached he seemed to have a 'glow' that caused listeners to be drawn to Christ. That was so in church, and also in open-air meetings where sometimes less than friendly crowds stopped to listen. He has been instrumental in bringing multitudes to Christ.

The first time I saw what I now know was a manifestation of the glory of God, was when I accidentally walked into a room where Jim was on his knees praying. I would describe what I saw that day, as either waves, or steam currents oscillating and rising from a road bathed in sunshine after rain. God's presence enveloped him, and touched me. I couldn't speak. I wanted to apologise for interrupting him but I was overwhelmed, so I backed out and closed the door. It's a hallowed memory that will always be with me. So when Jim speaks in this book about being visited by angels and having miraculous encounters with God, you can believe him!

To know Jim McConnell, is to know that he loves The Lord Jesus Christ supremely. Its obvious he has an intimate relationship with Christ, that's the result of hours of daily prayer and studying the Scriptures. When thousands of people in Ireland flocked to auditoriums and football stadiums to hear him preach, the press took notice that Jim McConnell was a local pastor. So they kept asking: "What's your secret?" Here's my answer: "God chose to call and mightily anoint him with The Holy Spirit, and he chose to stand on the words of Jesus; 'if I be lifted up from the earth, will draw all men unto me.' (John 12:32) And for over half a century that partnership has impacted Ireland and much of the world."

As a little girl, my wife Debby was led to Christ under Jim's ministry and spent her early years in his home as a friend of his daughter Linda. When we were married, the pastor, who officiated at our ceremony gave us an amazing prophetic word: "You will reach more people through your writing than in all the years of your preaching." That's pretty specific and leaves no wiggle room. At that time I was booked for the next two years to speak in churches across America, and I confess I didn't pay much attention to it. But like Mary, who 'hid these things in her heart', Debby wrote it down and dated it. And it came to pass. 'The Word For Today' daily devotional is now read in hard copy, heard on radio, and seen on television and internet platforms each day by an estimated 30 million people worldwide. To God be all the glory! And it started sixty years ago when Jim McConnell gave an altar call at the end of his sermon in a tiny wooden church in East Belfast, and I said yes to Jesus.

This book contains great Scriptural insights, records the highs and lows of ministry, and is a testament to what God can do with a life that's totally dedicated to Him. Do yourself a favour. Invest in your own spiritual growth by reading it, and invest in a friend or loved one by giving them a copy.

Bob Gass
Author, The Word For Today

INTRODUCTION

As I sit down to write this book, with a little help from my friends, I realise that my commitment to God and His people has never changed – it's all or nothing!

Each word in this book has been scripted from either the pain or joy of the journey in my sixty years in ministry. Whether learning to follow the voice of God, or writing about those moments personally that we all would find it difficult to talk about – it's all within these pages.

Scripture says; '*All things work together for the good to them that love God.*' Romans 8:28. Did you notice it does not state, only good things work together... but ALL things. This includes the good and the bad.

I was amused when the publisher presented me with the title of the book, '*The Good, The Bad and Jesus Christ!*' I realised, how true it is!

You see, our lives are normally divided into two avenues - there is the good, and then there is the bad. But as believers, we have Jesus Christ who can take what we deem as 'bad' and turn it around to make it good.

When I look back at my life and the times I fought like Joseph to get out of a bad situation, it was those days that made me realise that God had created a means of escape which is only found in Him.

As I share with you some of the stories that carved my life and character. I want to take you past the 'headlines' that you may have heard to the content of the story.

If I can help pastors or believers to run the race through the situations we all face without fear, then this book will be one treasure I seek to leave behind.

For the next number of pages allow me to minister to you.

Grace for the journey,

Pastor James McConnell

Chapter One

WHISTLING IN THE DARK

I was born in East Belfast on 15th May 1937. Yes I am that old! We lived at 14 Spring Street on the Woodstock Road. My father Edward was a driller in the famous Harland and Wolff shipyard, which employed over 30,000 men in its day and my mother Jean was a great housewife, building her wee family in what was known as a 'kitchen house.'

In those days in Belfast as World War II came near a close, the American GIs, the British soldiers and our local battalions were stocking up for the famous D-Day invasion. Due to the importance of Harland and Wolff to the war effort, the German Luftwaffe sought to flatten Belfast. During those times I remember my dad lifting my sister and me out of our beds and wheeling us in a pram quickly in the dark to the Castlereagh Hills. When the 'all clear' siren sounded, it was only then dad would lead us back to our home and thankfully, it was still standing.

I had a happy early childhood but sadly, I lost my mother at the age of eight. She developed septicaemia and passed away.

I am not sure whether it was the passing of my mum at such a young age that sparked off the fight against fear in my life, or if it was being moved basically overnight to live with my granny and granddad due to my sister's illness. But I know this - fear began a vicious fight to control me and to hold me hostage to its command.

Faith and fear are two opposites, and yet, each of them has a plan for you! Fear will seek to control you, it will cause you to dread getting out from under the bedsheets in the morning. It will cause you to not attend that job interview, it will cause you to lose your joy, but did you know faith has a plan?

When the armies of God were promised the land, fear's plan was for them to stay where they were, but faith's plan was to enter the promised land. As a young boy I did not realise this, for I had not yet met God. But somehow I knew at the other side of fear there is freedom and if nothing else, a new found confidence could be mine if I could be free from the fear! For instance, and this might make you smile – one night I decided to take a short-cut through an entry, leading from Cherryville Street to the old field at Spring Street. To stop the Luftwaffe seeing where the city was located, at night the people of Belfast were under orders to keep the city street lights switched off. The darkness of the night had captivated the streets. I remember gazing down that dark entry and thinking, there could be an assailant waiting on me, but James McConnell decided to walk the walk, and off I went into the darkness.

Like David lifting the five stones to face his Goliath, I lifted what was the next best thing - two half bricks! As David ran to his Goliath, I walked nervously; like Elvis, with a shake in the leg. My eyes glanced from side to side, the knuckles of my fingers were white from holding the bricks tight with fear, and then halfway into the entry I thought I noticed something. I began whistling in the dark. I'm not sure if it was a proper tune, or just a stammering whistle, but what I realised was, fear had made a tune.

It's wonderful how we see fear, and yet the very same situation in front of us can be seen differently when faith is at the wheel. I still sometimes find when I am nervous or anxious over some great decision, I start to hear a faint whistle. I then remember, I don't have two half bricks any longer in my hands, but something greater - the Word of God in my heart! Little did I know back then, as a young boy, that life's journey can sometimes take us down a dark path like that entry. It's a path that we ourselves would not have chosen, but nevertheless the path has been taken and we must walk along it.

That path of darkness can be a divorce, a break-up, the doctor telling you that you have cancer, a bankruptcy order, your child being admitted to hospital and the doctor saying: "There is nothing more we can do." It's that path that we are all frightened of, yet occasionally it just comes knocking on our door and we must learn to answer the call.

My beloved mother...

For several years I had the privilege of having my mum at my side. Her main desire was to keep me out of trouble and guide me down the right path in life. I loved my mother very much. She used to go to Greenisland to visit a girl called Minnie who was very wealthy and often, I'd accompany her. We were only a humble family living in a small house, but she and this lady were really made for each other. Together they formed a special relationship and when I look back now, I can see the impact that it had on me as a boy – I too sought that special relationship.

I remember meeting her a few years after my mum died and she said to me: "I miss your mother, she loved the simple things in life."

My mum was lovely - a wee stout lady who was very kind and popular with people. I was a restless wee boy and I think at times, I nearly had her head turned!

One day we were walking along the Albertbridge Road in Belfast and my mum noticed a policeman. She took my hand and walked over to him. I saw her winking at him and she said: "Talk to him and tell him he has to be a good boy!" Whether it was his voice or the uniform, I could feel my body shaking in front of this policeman, who was talking to me. But it taught me one thing – that my mother had an authority over me, but this policeman was elevated to a more senior level of authority. It is important to know whose authority one is under. Scripture says; *'For me and my house, we will serve the LORD.'* Joshua 24:15. Honouring our parents is a reflection of how we honour the Lord.

My mum's passing was a hugely significant moment in my life. It still is today, all these years later. I think about her every day. I remember the day she died. I came home from school and the neighbours were waiting on me and they told me the news. She died on 19th June - the close of World War II.

Mum died whilst pregnant with her third baby which was late in life for her. Septicaemia had set in and she died in agony. My last vivid memory of my mum was the birthday party she held for me; I had just turned eight. It is vivid in my mind. The kids were queued outside the house; she made everything, the food was amazing. A few days later, it was just after the war. They were having parties on the streets and I remember she came down the stairs and said to me: "Son, go and fetch Peggy Allen." She sat down on the stairs and I could see she was in pain. I ran down to Peggy who lived two doors down.

The ambulance came and took her away and that was the last I saw of my mum. She died shortly after she arrived in hospital; I later found out she died an agonising death. In those days when a woman was pregnant it was hidden from the children so I didn't understand what was wrong with my mum. Peggy was a very close friend and neighbour, and soon after my mum died she moved to England.

Two years after my mum passed away, both my father and Lila my sister who was fourteen, developed tuberculosis and the home was locked up. They were admitted to hospital so I was sent to live with my grandparents. Back in those days, it was called 'the bug.' I remember before they left having a separate cup and plate, and a separate knife and fork and we washed those well to have them ready for the next meal. As a child this would have an impact again, psychologically. It was like the lepers in the Bible - everything had to be cleansed once they touched it and people were told to stay away.

It's sad that we can still do this today as Christians. If people don't fit into our box or our thinking, the result is - we excommunicate them, we cross the road when we see the person coming or we look the other way - but love will never do this. In fact, Jesus the supreme manifestation of love, left Heaven to come down here to this sinful earth to save a wretch like James McConnell. And in the midst of the turmoil and darkness in my young life I was about to find that out!

Now living with my grandparents and attending Park Parade School, they had a difficult job managing me, and because I felt alone, I used to walk the streets at night until 2am. They gave me a key and I was able to get into the house and sometimes I didn't return until the next morning because I found a sanctuary in Ormeau Park. It wasn't that I was a troublesome child. But when I look back it was just that I wanted to be on my own. It is wonderful how the mind of a child works. Perhaps somewhere inside of me I had concluded that if I was by myself then I couldn't be hurt again, no-one could leave me again, especially those whom I loved. However, God had different plans, let's read...

Psalms 139:7-18;

'Whither shall I go from thy spirit? or whither shall I flee from thy presence? If I ascend up into heaven, thou art there: if I make my bed in hell, behold, thou art there. If I take the wings of the morning, and dwell in the uttermost parts of the sea; even there shall thy hand lead me, and thy right hand shall hold me. If I say, Surely the darkness shall cover me; even the night shall be light about me. Yea, the darkness hideth not from thee; but the night shineth as the day: the darkness and the light are both alike to thee. For thou hast possessed my reins: thou hast covered me in my mother's womb. I will praise thee; for I am fearfully and wonderfully made: marvellous are thy works; and that my soul knoweth right well. My substance was not hid from thee, when I was made in secret, and curiously wrought in the lowest parts of the earth. Thine eyes did see my substance, yet being unperfect; and in thy book all my members were written, which in continuance were fashioned, when as yet there was none of them. How precious also are thy thoughts unto me, O God! how great is the sum of them!

If I should count them, they are more in number than the sand: when I awake, I am still with thee.'

No matter where we seek to run or hide from God... when God has a call on your life... we must answer that call and it was during the summer nights as I slept under a big fir tree in Ormeau Park, God was going to be knocking on James McConnell's door.

Christ became so real to me. During those particular four years, while it was a disaster in my life, it was also a foundation for my life. I experienced the supernatural. The person I talked to most over those four years was Jesus. To Him - nobody else. In fact, He was more real to me then and He is more real to me today than human beings are.

Shortly after my father left hospital, he died of cancer. I remember before he passed away, I was rubbing his back because he was in pain and I recall him saying: "You are going to be an evangelist."

I think he knew something was going on in my life. Sadly, I hadn't been as close to him as I had been to my mother as his illness had separated me from him.

As I begin to take you on my journey know He who has started a good work in you is well able to finish it.

Chapter Two

MY FIRST ENCOUNTER

I became born again one Sunday afternoon in 1945 in the Iron Hall: the independent, evangelical church. I knelt down beside an old wooden bench at the age of eight and gave my heart and my life to the Lord. My Sunday School teacher, Sammy Jamison pointed me to Christ.

I had been attending the Iron Hall for several months and every time the doors would open, I would be there. Sammy would faithfully tell me about Jesus each Sunday, who He was, what He did and God's plan of Salvation. It was there young James McConnell gave his life to the Lord.

My grandfather had been an elder in the Iron Hall, so that's where my roots were. Even my mother used to take me there occasionally when she was alive during the war years and I remember the sailors coming into the Iron Hall in uniform, home on leave, so I had great affection for the church.

My first supernatural experience was when I was living at home in Spring Street. It was nearly Christmas and like a number of churches each year at this time, they would give out what were called, *Sunday School prizes*. The prize I received was a book about William Carey; the cobbler, missionary and Baptist minister who God sent to India.

I was really inspired by this book as William told how he had fallen from a tree and broke his leg yet his first desire was to go back to that tree and climb it again. This spoke to me, as it was then I realised that was the type of determination that I needed. I was inspired by his bravery and I remember the huge impact he had on me. His commitment to God and his desire to be totally 'sold out' led me in the middle of the night to kneel at my bedside and cry onto the Lord: "Lord I will go wherever you want me to go," and He revealed himself to me that very night.

As I knelt by my bed, my small room that was lit by a gas mantle was engulfed with rays of intense brightness - The presence of the Lord had entered my room! I had been praying and when I lifted my head up I saw what looked like a man standing in the middle of my bedroom looking down on me. I knew that he was an angel of the Lord. He told me that God's hand was upon me and that I had to live cleanly before him. He said that he would use me. With His assurance that He would be with me, I knew God had His hand on my life. As Scripture states; '*...I will pour out my spirit upon all flesh; and your sons and your daughters shall prophesy, your old men shall dream dreams, your young men shall see visions: and also upon the servants and upon the handmaids in those days will I pour out my spirit.*' Joel 2:28.

The experience in my room is as real to me today as it was back then. Some people may find that difficult to believe, sad to say even Christians. However, I have concluded that God has to be more than a so-called airy-fairy object in Heaven. He is our Creator who seeks to make Himself real to you, more than some of us want Him to be. This has been my experience and it has formed part of the foundation of my life and it can be yours too – God is real!

Seven times over my life an angel of the Lord has appeared to me and each time these supernatural encounters happened, the Holy Spirit anointed me to be able to stand before that person and to hear what he wanted me to do.

Listen carefully... You cannot believe in God and not believe in the supernatural for have you not read that Jesus multiplied the fish and bread? (Matthew 14) That's the supernatural! He healed the sick - (Mark 1) Supernatural! He raised the dead – (John 11) Supernatural! And to defeat the root of fear we must understand that the God we serve is the God of the supernatural!

Even God had to convince the disciples that He Himself was supernatural. Have you read about the type of disciples Jesus picked? Seriously, if they were applying for the position of a pastor nowadays, do you think they would stand a chance of being successful?

These men, most of whom were professionals in their own trade, had no understanding of the supernatural – if they did, they would have known where to catch the fish! (Luke 5:5) But what did Jesus do? He told them to let the net down in the heat of the day, at a time when it was virtually impossible to catch fish. What was Jesus doing? He was introducing them to the supernatural. For that to happen, He walked with them, fellowshipped with them, ate with them, lived with them and all for one purpose... He wanted God to be more than a word but a living experience. And that was my introduction to God... in a small room in the middle of the night He came!

From that first night I felt a strong call on my life and I had from then on, a real desire to preach and read. I just devoted my time to reading - I loved the Bible. My favourite portions of Scripture were 1st and 2nd Samuel and the Gospels. I remember reading the books of Samuel from my grandfather's large Bible.

Reading was a great challenge to me. As a young boy I had no interest in school. I just wanted to be a footballer. I attended school sometimes, but never took an interest in any of the classes. I was seen as just a bit 'thick' but I wasn't bothered. I thought I had no prospects, so why bother? However from that encounter in my bedroom, my motivation became clear. Now I had an overwhelming desire to learn all about God's Word, His character and His commands. I wanted to learn all I could and was desperate to do so.

The Bible tells us; '*For ye see your calling, brethren, how that not many wise men after the flesh, not many mighty, not many noble, are called: but God hath chosen the foolish things of the world to confound the wise; and God hath chosen the weak things of the world to confound the things which are mighty; and base things of the world, and things which are despised, hath God chosen, yea, and things which are not, to bring to nought things that are: that no flesh should glory in his presence.*' 1 Corinthians 1:26-29.

Sometimes I just thank God for this verse because it qualifies the unqualified and that was me, James McConnell. I am so glad that God does not look for a university graduate, for if He did, I likely would not have been in ministry. But I will tell you what He does look for - he seeks out a heart that is available to change under Him.

As a young boy I had no hope of achieving anything, but God kept creating a deep desire within me to study His Word. And this hunger caused me to read the Bible. I wanted to know what the Bible told me about Christ. That was all I was interested in. I studied in my house, I even got up in the middle of the night to read. I read in my bed and at breakfast. I was reading everywhere.

Speaking in a new language...

I remember one day I was walking down the brick footpath along the Ravenhill Road, making my way to school. My mind was overtaken by consuming concerns. I tried to shove them to the back of my head but they relentlessly pursued until I finally gave in to the chorus of doubts and fears. The facts laid my soul bare. I was fourteen years old. I had just buried my father. I was alone. The weight of the truth lay evidently across my shoulders.

Who was there to guide me? Whose name could I call upon

for help? I was a mere boy thrust into premature manhood, and I knew that whatever I did then would affect the rest of my life, like permanent ink upon the crisp white pages of a fine book.

Tears began to roll down my cheeks as evidence of a cry I could not suppress. The grief, the pain and the loss mingled together like a widow's tapestry. Yet, something began to stir within the depths of my soul, a feeling of life that I could not shift, life that stood defiantly against the despair and death. With a resounding and triumphant song, I cried out to God and began to sing;

'Face to face with Christ my Saviour,
face to face what will it be?
When the rapture I behold Him,
Jesus Christ who died for me.'

I hadn't even noticed the familiar sight of Park Parade Secondary School, it's brown brick walls and white window frames standing in the not so far distance, nor the sound of my peers making their way to class. The world around had melted into insignificance as this song poured forth out of my mouth. Consumed by praise, my heart swelling with joy, I was unexpectedly swept up in another language. What was happening to my body was completely foreign to me, I started speaking out words I did not understand. I was talking loudly, yet flowing beautifully with an affluent grace! How could I express these events, such things that even the world's brightest communicators would struggle to summarise. Jesus was the one who cried out; *'If any man thirst, let him come unto me, and drink. He that believeth on me, as the scripture hath said, out of his belly shall flow rivers of living water.'* John 7:37-38

His Word was being made manifest.

It was as if God was ensuring my day was captivated by Him, as if He was determined that I was not to escape. I walked into school where my first class was music, a favourite for the boys who loved the talented young Welsh teacher. Traditionally she favoured the classic composers, Bach or Schubert. The previous week we covered Royal favourite, La Rejouissance by Handel, the piece made famous by the great fireworks display commissioned by George II. This day however, she looked down at her notes, then stared at the class sitting silently. "We're going to break our tradition today and try something a little different," she said. "Hopefully you will all recognise this hymn... Abide with me."

My knees buckled beneath me. I could feel my heart welling up once again. The room around me chorused the song in time with our dear teacher, most of them droning out the words with about as much emotion as an oven mitt. But here I was, worshipping my King once again, an already drenched soul thrown back into the neck-deep waters. It was too much. My resolve couldn't withstand the intensity of God's Spirit. My knees finally gave away and I slumped onto my desk as my eyes began to stream with an unending flow of tears. I grabbed fistfuls of my school jersey and started scrubbing at my face, wiping away my tears as the flow of the Holy Spirit continued to overpower me.

I felt the hand of another boy against my shoulder, and a whisper in my ear: "What's the matter with you? Are you sick?" I recognised the familiar sound of the friend I played football with. I could hear a couple more whispering as the teacher played away, the last verse nearing conclusion. A strength foreign to my own body filled me from head to toe, I wiped away some more tears and confessed: "I feel great!"

There was no going back, He was empowering me and preparing me, I was *never* going to be the same again.

Planting pots...

Even though the Bible teaches clearly on the Baptism of the Holy Spirit, the Iron Hall where I attended did not accept this. They believed that was just for the time relating to the Book of Acts. Somehow they tried to say, God had done away with the Baptism of the Holy Spirit at the end of the Book of Acts. With all my studying of the Word of God, I felt this was incorrect but they disagreed with me, even though the pastor of the church kept his own filling of the Holy Spirit private.

But while men may seek to hinder you from the move of God, He began to open my spiritual eyes to show me that it was never Him who changed but the church. Scripture says; *'Jesus Christ the same yesterday, and today, and for ever.'* Hebrews 13:8

The Book of Acts records the start of the outpouring of the Holy Spirit on the church but nowhere does it record it stopped. Because it is God's express will for us to live in Him through the baptism of the Holy Spirit. The question is then, why should you or I allow any man to stop us entering into the fullness of God through the Baptism of the Holy Spirit? I had no other option but to stop going to the Iron Hall.

I decided to attend a little hall called the Bible Pattern Church. The people who attended were lovely to me. It was a small church, consisting of about thirty people. Because I was one of the younger kids and they were quite elderly, they were so kind to me, and they spoiled me. It was later that I realised God had used them to take me out of a smaller planting pot and into a larger one.

Let me not mince my words here… but really, how well do you want to grow in the understanding of God? Remember a tree can only grow to the depth and the surrounds in which it has been placed, and the Bible calls us the *'trees of righteousness'* Isaiah 61:3.

What type of soil are you spiritually planted into? Is it too dry? – No Spirit moving? Too wet? – No solid teaching? Cramped? – No room for your 'gifts' to come alive in the Holy Spirit? For me I found out the roots of the righteous tree God had planted in me had reached the boundaries (the doctrines) of the Iron Hall I was previously in. Whether I liked it or not, I had realised for me to grow in God I had to come out of the smaller container and so I joined The Bible Pattern Church.

At the age of 13 I stood up at the front of The Bible Pattern Church and delivered my first sermon in a wee pulpit with frills around it. The sermon was called, 'The Sufferings of Christ,' and it was based on Psalm 22. I talked about how I was amazed that 1000 years before the piercing of the Lord's hands and feet happened, the Psalmist David saw it being fulfilled. That really captured me. The sermon lasted for ten minutes and I shook like a leaf but the ladies of the church encouraged me. They thought I was the best thing since penicillin!

To prepare my sermons, I used to pray and preach them to myself. I used to preach aloud to myself in Ormeau Park, then write everything down, so it would be easy to follow, once I was in the pulpit.

Chapter Three

TAKING ON A TRADE

A certain man called William Towel, was very good to me and he also was a member of the Bible Pattern Church. An evangelist by heart, at every opportunity he told people about Jesus, and when a new apprentice would start at the Harland and Wolff shipyard where he worked, he would give them a free New Testament. Sadly, he has gone now to be with the Lord. William and his wife Lily were wonderful people.

That morning as I was leaving school, he asked me: "What are you going to do Jim? What trade are you going to have?" Well I hadn't a clue. What was I going to do? I knew God's hand was on me and I wanted to be in the ministry, but I was too young.

I was fifteen, so William got me a job training to be a plumber. At that time, to be a plumber you had to pay five pounds. That was the rule of Harland and Wolff back then. Plumbing was a trade and you had to pay the fee. I remember the big white fivers; if I'd owned one, I would have framed it! I recall gathering rubbish from all the alleyways to try to save up enough money. You got four pence per bucket, but I later learned that William paid the fee for me behind my back. When you believe in someone you invest in them! Don't get me wrong here, investment is not always about money… something that can be more important is 'time!' When I look back it was never the money that made the impact on me – it was an investment of 'time' that people gave me… my parents, my grandparents and now William; each one helped me enter a new season in my life.

When God wants to bring you into a new realm in your life and in many instances your spiritual walk, He will bring a person into your life to help you be guided into the promise He has given to you. Consider Elisha, he had Elijah. Joshua had Moses, Timothy had Paul, Jesus had John the Baptist where the heavens opened, and Mary had Elizabeth.

When I arrived on my first day at Harland and Wolff to start my plumbing trade, it would seem the bosses had other plans for me. They wanted me to stay in the office and become a clerk. They told me I would receive a decent salary and enjoy a job for life, so I didn't pursue plumbing. The men at the shipyard were big, tough characters, but they knew my dad had died and that my sister was in hospital. They were ungodly men, but they were the best ungodly men I had ever met in my life! They were so generous to me, holding a weekly collection to help out every Friday. After they collected the money they bought a list of groceries and sweets for my sister, which I delivered to her on the Saturday. Those men could really teach a few Christians what charity is!

Through William I noticed a 'path' had started to reveal itself in my life, and would continue on into my sixty years of ministry – God would bring 'key' people into my life and in turn they would help me unlock the next stage of my walk in Him.

My sister was very ill at that time and for those four and a half years that she was in hospital, I roamed the streets. I felt very alone. My mother was dead and my father, while alive, gave my sister all his attention because she was in hospital. I spent my time in the park, hiding away there, because it was my secret place. Even the park attendants never saw me. Nobody knew where I was, I was hidden from view. Those days and nights alone in Ormeau Park, was God training me for His call over my life.

Pastors have a Sunday life and then a Monday life. A Sunday is where they get to share the wondrous Gospel of Jesus Christ to their congregation, and it's amazing! But then Monday comes. Monday is the day when the rubber hits the road, the day when praise can arrive on your desk, along with an envelope called loneliness!

Yes, it's that subject pastors dread to talk about but sadly if not dealt with, can destroy you. How many of us battle with loneliness? For me, I found loneliness to be an education. It's an exam that you have to pass, to win honours and to become strong and wise.

What I have under the tree is precious. It's real, and it's strengthening! I will still be there when I'm eighty. It is the trysting place between me and my beloved Master who early on, became my father and my mother, my sister and my brother. I would be lost without Him now, as I would have been years ago.

Do you have a tree?

I still go every day to Ormeau Park. The tree I sat at is bare now because the years have taken their toll. At that time, it was surrounded by barbed wire, and large signs stating: 'Trespassers Will Be Prosecuted' and 'Poison.' As trespassing was prohibited, I was more determined to find a way in. When no-one was looking I would climb over the fence. For a young lad, it was like an adventure playground, except these were real tanks and guns, all for the war effort, and they were being made ready to be transported to the frontline. That was the sort of boy I was. I hated to be hemmed in and I still do now.

I call Ormeau Park my trysting place, my altar. The Whitewell folks laugh because if something happens and I take them to the park, then they are either in trouble or they are going to receive a blessing! There are many different types of people who know what Ormeau Park means to me. And there are times when some great crisis comes into their life and they ask me to take them there and talk to them. But I am careful not to show them *the* tree – I show them the trees!

It is that secret place which will cause us to attain separation from the 'things' of this world into the hidden place where He has called us to. If we choose to keep entering then our life will never be the same again.

Have you got a secret place? The Bible speaks very clearly about entering into the secret place, a place that is kept secret, but do you know why? The way by which the Lord will lead you into His presence may not be the exact same way that He will lead me or someone else. He does not want you to be a copycat, He wants you to be an original! Each of us needs to find that so-called 'tree' in our life and learn to build a campfire of prayer and fasting around it. Don't misread me here… the secret is not '*the tree*.' It is '*but a tree*.' Likewise, it was not Moses' rod, nor the jaw bone that Samson used, or the handkerchief that Paul prayed on. The secret is entering in, hearing what the Lord is saying to you - which is found in the secret place.

This could be your bedroom, the car, a chair, a mountain, a walk, beside the river – only you will know and when you find it – make a habit of entering and camping at it… as Moses to the bush, he was drawn to it… you too will be brought forth. We must not seek to work it out in our minds - we must only obey.

A lady in my church, Nellie Garner, a real saint, called me one day and she said: "Brother Jim, keep the secret of the Lord!" Friends, find that 'secret place', enter it and make a habit of living your life from it. If you have no secret place – Create one!

Preaching, is it an art?

My quiet time is very important to me. I pray, read and write every day. My thinking is, a day is wasted if I don't. I have always shut myself away and spent time focusing on the written Word.

When I was younger, I used to keep a wee notebook in my car; when I eventually got a car it was an MG, a battered one! It only took me thirteen years to do so. When a thought popped into my head I would stop the car and write it down. Most days I write for about four hours. Some days I scribble and other days I write something that is really special. I really do gain inspiration from many sources. It's amazing, as even in the middle of stuff that you think is nonsense, there can be a wee gold nugget there.

Sometimes I just turn over a new page and start with a text from the Bible. I write the text down and ask myself - if I was reading this passage for the first time, what would I say about it? Then as I start to answer that question, it all becomes clear. It explodes onto the page. The Holy Spirit will introduce ideas to you. He will bring things to your remembrance.

When I was working in the drawing office, they allowed me to read the Bible there. The directors used to laugh at me reading as they couldn't understand why a fifteen-year-old boy would sit down and read the Bible, instead of comic books or magazines. They were fascinated at me annotating the Bible in different colours - red, yellow and green - to highlight different passages. Even when I am preaching now, I can still see that Bible sitting in front of me. I even mark my sermons similarly, and preachers have copied me. Great preachers, better preachers than me have copied my method. It got to the stage where my Bible was all colours. It was my technicolour Bible - a rainbow Bible that glowed in the dark!

I read and I prayed. I used to walk the roads and I would pray aloud to God: "Lord will you make my mind like blotting paper? That everything I read I will absorb!" The Lord Jesus said that the Holy Spirit would bring all things to our remembrance.

Jesus Christ said; *"But the Comforter, which is the Holy Ghost, whom the Father will send in my name, he shall teach you all things, and bring all things to your* ***remembrance****, whatsoever I have said unto you."* John 14:26

Now to remember everything, you have either got to hear it, read it or see it. So I read it. And when I read, I also prayed: "Lord make my mind like a sponge that I will absorb everything that I read."

I was able to memorise the four Gospels. I tried to learn a little bit of Hebrew and Greek. I wasn't brilliant at that but I learned some words. I took it from a colleague of mine who bought the Reader's Digest. It had a section in it at that time where you learned a word. I began with one word every month. I read that word and memorised it - in a bid to increase my vocabulary and to learn the meanings. I taught myself. I didn't attend Bible College or university. In fact, I skipped school quite a lot because I was too busy in the park. That was my training ground. I tried my best with the Hebrew and Greek, but my pronunciation of the words was appalling. Having said that, sometimes stubbornness is good - I stuck to it and I learned it!

There is nothing in the Word of God that is there by accident, and if this is so, then each word, each sentence, each chapter must be treated as of extreme importance.

We just read the word 'remembrance' in John 14:26. Remembrance may not come when you expect it, it may not be all at once, but when you are going through some difficulty or some circumstance or a trial that is when He will bring something to your remembrance.

When I used to watch University Challenge, I noticed the students at the start of each programme would introduce themselves: "My name is so and so, and I am reading Mathematics." Or: "I am reading Philosophy."

I used to think that everybody was reading, but I remember asking myself: "What is James McConnell reading?" It was very difficult to enjoy reading when education was not my strong point.

Even though I had missed out in schooling to a degree, I decided not to miss out on God and what He could do for me. My conclusion was, if God took time to write the Bible, then surely God is wanting us to read it! So, I started building my library and began to spend all my pocket money on books.

Chapter Four

NAME IN THE 'BLACK BOOKS'

I have a great library but I hardly use it now. In the early days I used it a lot. I was like Spurgeon, when he started on Park Street. That was his first church in London before he built the Metropolitan Tabernacle in London. He was one of the finest preachers the world has ever seen, I named our church in memory of him. If one reads his sermons carefully and his headings, it's clear he has been inspired by Matthew Henry. He took Henry's headings or as I call them coat hangers and he put clothes on them, powerful stuff! My reading list every day was as follows - Matthew Henry exposition, a sermon by Spurgeon, an exposition by Joseph Parker, a character study by Alexander White and then a few years later I added George Henry Morrison to that. He was a Scottish preacher who was brilliant. Those were the ones that I cut my teeth on.

I saved up my money and bought the books. A man who owned a second-hand Bible shop during the 1960's would sell customers books on tick. At one point I owed him £400 which was a fortune back then. I had difficulty paying him back. He could acquire books that other shops didn't have. I remember one day there was a fire and most of the shop was destroyed, I said: "Praise God, so has the bill!" but he told me that he had two black books and my name was in both of them!

I think the seller took pity on me. He could see my desire to read so he let me have the books. I tried to pay him back, I would give him ten shillings at a time, but then when I was in the shop paying him, I would see another book and I'd want to add it to my collection. I was absorbed in all this great Bible teaching; I was so desperate to learn so I started buying all around me. I remember him giving me these great books, but they were full of creepy crawlies! I used to squash them in the pages! He encouraged me, he saw my enthusiasm and he saw I was hungry for God.

As soon as I received my wage from church, he was my first stop. Then after a while, I started to receive gifts of books which helped.

He used to ask me if I really wanted a particular book. I used to say yes, so he would give it to me but he still marked it down in his book. I remember buying a treasury of David from him and it was full of insects, absolutely crawling with them! I still read it today – But the insects are gone!

Measured blessings....

It is very important to develop a studying routine to grow strong in God's Word. Remember, regardless of what commentaries you read, or how many sermons you can digest, there is no shortcut to knowing the things of God. God's blessing isn't just poured out upon a person in one fell swoop, neither does He give you the keys to knowledge in one go. I don't even know if our fragile human minds would even be capable of retaining such depth without becoming compromised.

God does not bless you all at once, neither does He tell you everything at once. He will lead you step by step – there are no short-cuts to His success, He takes you by the long road. Our step by step walk with God cannot go underrated or unappreciated. It is through our journeys, the long and winding wilderness roads, where we have His truth implanted into our very lives. It is known that God could have led His people through the quick and easy route to the Promised Land. Exodus 13:18 says; *'But God led the people about, through the way of the wilderness.'* It wasn't that His map was wrong or that the GPS was broken, God knows the paths in which He takes us! The path of His servant is to travel the hard and barren wastelands. It is here where God meets with us face to face to write His Word directly onto our hearts. This is what was awaiting me, just as it awaits every person who has been ordained for His purposes.

If the Lord has called you to preach then prepare your notes and practice! Never let arrogance take you to the forefront of the battle before your time. This is where I take myself off and I preach away to those trees in Ormeau Park! Also show humility - The mirror image should never be a reflection of you but of Christ. As it says in Luke 9:48; '*...for he that is least among you all, the same shall be great.*' Humility is the hidden ingredient in grace. It is the hinge that opens the door that no flesh can touch – grace. It is never how big we can become; it is how big JESUS can become in us. When you look in the mirror, never ask yourself how big am I? The question is, how small am I? We need only be 'seed size' to move mountains! (Matthew 17:20).

The wrapping must match the gift...

Remember in your gifting – The wrapping paper must match the gift! The Bible says in Proverbs 18:16; '*A man's gift maketh room for him, and bringeth him before great men.*' Wrap the gift in you with what suits it the best! A plumber carries a spanner, a carpenter a saw. I carried a library within! What do you carry? Stir up that 'gift' by reading and studying what you are called to do. To be a good craftsman study and walk beside someone who is good at it!

As the vocation entails, many times I am met by pastors and ministers of other churches where we sit together and chat over a cup of tea. It isn't long before the conversation swings in the direction of last Sunday's sermon, where I'm asked what I preached, how it was received, where did I feed my thoughts from, and a popular question is always: "How do you keep your sermons so fresh?" It isn't a complicated procedure I can tell you that! What have you been reading? What have you got in your study library?

Time after time I hear of the malnourished bookshelves housing poor reading material. An underfed library implies an underfed minister - it takes fresh meat to produce fresh meat!

Regardless of what a man is before his congregation, when he is alone before God in his study, he is still a student learning the things of God. Our learning is never finished and so, God's book should never be out of his hand. We should constantly be studying to better our understanding of the things of God, and to improve ourselves, as Paul wrote to Timothy *'Study to shew thyself approved unto God, a workman that needeth not be ashamed, rightly dividing the word of truth.'* 2 Timothy 2:15

Our study habit affects our preaching abilities. It is essential that we are as nourished for preaching as we can be, given the importance of the task in light of scripture. Preaching is considered old-fashioned by many today but Paul directly ties it to the art of soul-winning. Think of all the countless evangelism programmes receiving attention and focus, yet this neglected method is the only one Paul considered worth mentioning in Romans 10 *'How then shall they call on him in whom they have not believed? And how shall they believe in him of whom they have not heard? And how shall they hear without a preacher? And how shall they preach, except they be sent? So then faith cometh by hearing, and hearing by the word of God.'*

He says again to Timothy; *'Preach the word; be instant in season, out of season; reprove, rebuke, exhort with all longsuffering and doctrine. For the time will come when they will not endure sound doctrine; but after their own lusts shall they heap to themselves teachers, having itching ears; and they shall turn away their ears from the truth, and shall be turned unto fables.'* 2 Timothy 4:2-4

Well, what does this verse tell us about the modern fascination with non-preaching? That the time has come to deliver the Word of God!

One of the problems faced by certain pastors is the lack of

assistance. Pastors are frequently distracted by all sorts of jobs that take them away from their role of preparing good sermons for their people. The ability and opportunity to delegate other responsibilities is essential. Acts 6, is the first example of administrative delegation in the Early Church, paralleling the wisdom and principle of Moses' decision to employ judges (Exodus 18:13-27). Just like the Apostles realised, pastors need to be free to be given to the Word of God and prayer.

A pastor who can overcome these issues and begin to carefully, prayerfully, and studiously prepare sermons, and preach them by the power of the Holy Spirit will be rewarded. People are hungry to hear the Word of God regardless of what the world has to say. John 10:27 tells us; *'My sheep hear my voice, and I know them, and they follow me.'*

How sensitive are you to following in God's steps? Do we follow at a distance, do we follow closely or do we actually watch what steps He is taking, for the path specifically laid out for us and enter into those steps? Each one a different level of grace and authority. How closely are you following?

Man in the tea cosy...

Let me share with you a particular experience I will never forget. I was working away, serving my time as a message boy in the drawing office. I knew I would have to do that for a few years before I could climb the ladder. It was my first proper job and I really enjoyed it. At that time Harland and Wolff was recognised world-wide for their shipbuilding and offshore construction.

One morning, I remember it well - it was November 9, 1954, I was sitting at my desk. This man came towards me. He was wearing a 'tea cosy' hat and a long duffle coat with wooden buttons.

I said to him: "Good morning."

He said: "Good morning, look this way."

I turned and he said to me: "What do you see?"

I said: "I see a warehouse."

He said: "What else do you see?"

I said: "I see a man in the warehouse with a ridiculous-looking little can and he is pouring oil into big vessels, wee vessels and medium-sized vessels."

He said: "You saw correctly, now it's up to you which vessel you are going to be. Good morning."

He walked through the swing doors and disappeared and that was it. I got up and ran after him. But it took me a while to realise what had happened to me. I was in a daze. It's like when Peter left prison and he was in the street, or the story of the prodigal son – the Bible says he came to his senses. (Acts 12:11, Luke 15:11-32)

When I came to my senses and realised what had happened, I ran through the swing doors and into the Chief Executive, Sir Frederick Rebbeck's office. He was a good man, but a stern man. I was in awe of him.

I said: "I'm sorry sir."

He said: "You are alright son, who are you looking for?"

"I am looking for somebody," I said.

"Who is it?" He asked.

"I don't know," I replied.

He ushered me out of the way and said: "Away you go, away you go!" And that was it. I knew it had happened again - that the Lord had revealed Himself to me.

It was an amazing encounter and one I will never forget!

I returned to my desk and I leaned back in my chair, breathing in the moment and making it last as long as I could. My head nodded in agreement and understanding, yet I was shaken to the very core by the accuracy and truth which was now striking my innermost depths. I clasped my hands together and bowed my head, not caring who or what was watching, and acknowledged - God was in my life by the power of the Holy Spirit.

The Bible tells us in 2 Timothy 2:20; *'But in a great house there are not only vessels of gold and of silver, but also of wood and of earth; and some to honour, and some to dishonour.'*

Can I ask, what sort of vessel are you?

When Paul was writing about vessels in his time they were used for holding water, oil or wine. Symbolising the Holy Spirit. Are you an empty vessel? A half-filled vessel? Or an overflowing vessel of the Lord? If you want to know the will of God for your life, it is very simple… the will of God is that you should be filled by the Spirit. Every child of God should be a container full of the Spirit.

Apostle Paul was known in the Bible as being a chosen vessel. God had a purpose for his life. God said to Paul in Acts 9:15; *'He is a chosen vessel unto me.'* In the Greek it means, he is a vessel of election. He was called to do miracles, he was called to do great things but was also called to suffer. He was a vessel unto honour.

The Lord explained to me how this is what happens in His storehouse, He is the one who enters in and fills the vessels with the message of deliverance. The great and mighty vessels are unable to carry His oil as they are unyielding, lacking humility and a heart that waits on the Lord in His secret place. So, He pours out upon the little vessels, the weak ones of the world, and raises them with His great power.

He has looked upon you as He looks upon the little vessels. He has seen that you are weak in your own esteem and humbled before His throne. He sees that you have the heart and desire to serve Him, and so you will be one of those little vessels. If you are faithful in the capacity that has been given to you, He will grow you and fill you with Himself. You must do what you have been commanded to do.

Chapter Five

A CROWD OF ONE

The Bible had become a book of life to me. The 'doctrine' that was implanted in me in the Iron Hall was 'God is in Heaven and next time you will see Him, meet Him, experience Him is when you die!' That is of course, if you are born-again! But I was experiencing the God I shared with you earlier now on a regular basis – The book of Acts was and still is making stories. Are we one of those stories?

When my sister left hospital she lived with us in Spring Street for a short time, but tuberculosis had left her with various health problems. I rejoiced when my sister became saved in 1956 just after the Lord called me into ministry.

Pastor Gordon Magee held a mission in a band hall at Devon Parade in Sydenham and asked me to preach at it. Over the ten days, 250 people were crammed into the hall nightly and thirty-three people became born-again, baptised in water and filled with the Holy Spirit. Each one is still going strong with the Lord today. That was the mission of my lifetime because my sister became saved that night, as did Robert Gass and Sydney Murray.

I remember Sydney Murray was quite a character. He had served time for theft and had just been released from prison. Unfortunately he had become involved in thieving again. His wife

Lily was so fed up. She was scared he would be sent back to prison so she was ready to give up, as she had no hope for the future. I remember a few months before the mission I was crossing the Albertbridge Road and I saw Lily, who I knew from my childhood days.

She was standing at the bridge, holding her baby, poised and ready to throw herself over the bridge.

I shouted at her: "Lily, hold it! Wait! Please!" I knelt down and prayed for her on the bridge in the middle of the pouring rain.

I said to her: "We will win Sydney to Christ!"

So I was overjoyed when Sydney attended the mission that night and came to know the Lord. Every one of those people who became saved all started their journeys with the Lord. It was the best mission of my lifetime. Sydney continued to grow in the Lord and is now a great evangelist and has led many to Christ.

Robert Gass also got saved that night. He is now an international speaker and is the author of the popular, 'The Word For You Today'. He publishes over three million daily devotionals every quarter in many languages and adaptations. Bob is known for his inspiring, thought-provoking messages, and has authored over thirty books.

My wife Margaret's brother got saved at the same mission as did my sister Lila. I was delighted that I played a part in her coming to know Christ. With us being separated as children due to her illness, I really felt this was something that would tie us together. A shared love for the Lord. She was great, we had grown very close, she went on with the Lord and did well. Sadly she died shortly after that but I took comfort in knowing that she was going to be with her Saviour. I remember she was found dead sitting on the settee with an open Bible.

The lady with the flowing hair...

I knew from that first encounter in my bedroom that God had set out a path for me. I really felt a strong call of God on my life. This was confirmed to me one day by a powerful encounter I had in the Bible Pattern Church.

When I was attending the church, I was given a key to enable me to open up and put the heating on. I used to switch it on from 7.30am until 11pm each Sunday, with the result that the church was extremely hot. I am sure I cost them a fortune in heating bills! I did that every Sunday morning. I remember one particular morning though, I came in, switched on the heating and I locked the doors behind me.

After I did a few checks, I then knelt down by one of the pews and started singing to the Lord. I sang a hymn that I loved...

'Take my life and let it be;
consecrated, Lord, to Thee.
Take my moments and my days,
Let them flow in endless praise...'

Suddenly the locked doors burst open! This lady appeared in front of me. She had long flowing hair and she scared the life out of me! I was frozen to the spot.

I recognised her as a very wealthy lady who attended the church and she was driven everywhere by her chauffeur. She usually wore a large hat and always wore her hair up so I'd never seen her like this before. As she rushed in, her hair was flowing at the speed she was travelling at. She gave me quite a shock!

She came over to me and laid her hands on my shoulders and started prophesying. Let me just drop in here – prophesying is where you allow God to speak a word into your spirit man and then you release that word in season to the whoever.

She said: "You will go around the world. I will take you and I will use you. I will bless you."

After she prophesied, she walked out and that was that. She left church that morning and her chauffeur was waiting for her outside. This was about 8.30am. He drove her home and then she returned for the 11am service. Apparently the Lord told her to come and tell me that. I was fifteen then. Her words came to pass.

The call of God...

The call of God is special, it is above every other calling. There is nothing else to match the call of God. Whether you are working, whatever you are doing, when God calls you that is greater than anything else in your life. To be called by God is a prestigious promotion and an honour.

I knew from a young age that God had placed a call on my life but the prophecy given by this woman in the church simply confirmed it. Is there a call upon your life? If so, let Him use that call. In the Bible, Abraham's call was threefold, he was told; '*Get thee out of thy country, and from thy kindred, and from thy father's house.*' (Genesis 12:1) God was wanting total separation with Abraham. God told Abraham "Get ye out!" You would think God was from Northern Ireland with that type of statement!

An important thing to note about Abraham is that he was 75-years-old when he was called by God. You are never too young or too old to be called by God. The call of God is unique, totally different to any other calling. It demands total surrender. I think it is fantastic he was 75, I wish I had that energy! I remember we had a unique man in our congregation called John Patterson and he used to say to me: "Bishop, when you are 90, you are never the same!" This is so true as when you get old, every day is precious!

Twenty five years later, the call of God was totally fulfilled in Abraham's life. God's calling and commands are rarely accompanied with reasons but they are always accompanied with promises. He told Abraham: *'I will bless thee... and thou shalt be a blessing.'* (Genesis 12:2) You cannot be a blessing to anyone until God blesses you!

There are many believers that have a real desire to serve God, but there is a difference between a call and a desire. A call deserts every other desire. The man who is called of God, he doesn't lose it! If they lost the call then they hadn't been called at all. A man who is called of God does not *lose it* as God has ordained him and predestined him to do it.

The secret of true dedication lies in stamina; oh the people I know who fizzled out, others that started out well when I was a kid. I remember a pastor said to me one day: "Yes plenty of ups and downs but no ins and outs!" His words were so true, we must go steadily on with the Lord. There will be ups and downs but we can't give up. Quitters are those who lack stamina. If you have quit, get back to God and serve the Lord with all your heart! You need stamina to do the work of God right! Let's keep on going and keep on growing and the Lord will be with us.

The greatest trial for Abraham was when God put his finger on what he loved the most, Isaac. One more *wee* test for him was when He told him to take his son and offer him as a burnt offering. Abraham didn't argue, he rose up early in the morning and took Isaac on a three-day journey to Mount Moriah. Have you ever had a three-day journey with God? This is all part of dedication, all part of stamina.

There are pastors today, they phone me and they talk to me. They lack the stamina to do what is right. They do what is necessary but won't go an inch further. The Lord said to Abraham, I want your son. Their goal is the bare minimum; they have no interest in excellence. Excellence is above and beyond what is required. The greatest privilege in the world is to serve God and to follow His call in your life.

Chapter Six

CONTROVERSIAL MENTORS

True prophecy will always bring hope to our weary heart. With that message in the Bible Pattern Church, I was able to pick up and continue with that hope in mind. He is faithful to provide for all our needs. For me, and for others too, that will often require support. Jesus sent the disciples out in pairs, we are never abandoned to His work alone. Even though we may have times like Elijah where we feel like we are the only ones left, it is never that way.

God was faithful to provide two men in my life who I give thanks for. Often times they have been viewed as controversial, heretical at the extreme. These things are always a matter of opinion, and we have to be aware that even as servants of God we are never going to wholly avoid misrepresentation. I myself may speak of the role they have played in my life, of the encouragement I received from them as they discerned the grace of God in my life.

I remember in 1954, I met Pastors James Forsythe and Gordon Magee from the Church of God who were Godly men - that I cannot deny. When I was alone, they opened their homes. When I was in need, they shared love. Where I was weak, they strengthened me in wisdom and teaching. Isn't this the epitome of Christ-like love? There are many men in Northern Ireland and further afield who say they possess the truth, but when it comes to examining the fruit, it is clear that the preaching isn't applied in their daily lives, in their relationships and in their attitudes. We can only testify of what we have seen.

It was through James Forsythe that I learned how to pray and worship, and was able to grow in the practical side of God's work. The ability to communicate forthrightly came from the master in the craft of preaching, Gordon Magee. Gordon is undoubtedly one of the top ten preachers I have heard in my lifetime. He was a Godly man and was a marvellous blessing in my life. He taught me to develop my communication gift, and to be constructive in sermon preparation.

I left the Bible Pattern Church much to the disappointment of the people. They did everything to prevent me from leaving because they loved me but I knew it was time to move on. I needed to spread my wings and fly. As I grew in God I began to look for deeper things and the Spirit told me to go to the Church Of God. I had such dreams and desires to travel the world and lead multitudes to Christ. I couldn't see those things being fulfilled staying where I was.

George Jeffreys, the Welsh minister who founded the Bible Pattern Church and Elim Pentecostal Church and a preacher who I loved dearly, became interested in me and he wanted to bring me to Clapham Crescent in London. When I was about to leave their little Bible Pattern Church on My Ladys Road, he was their last trump card. They showed me letters from George, mentioning my name, praising the work I'd done there. They thought this would persuade me to stay.

Even though it was a controversial decision leaving the Bible Pattern Church, I went with these two men, James Forsythe and Gordon Magee to the Church of God. The people tried their very best to stop me going with them as they were wary of them – but that was a matter of opinion. These two men had the ability and the foresight to see the grace of God in my life and they gave me precious encouragement to pursue my ministry.

Gordon Magee was a real servant of God who taught me many things. I looked up to him but I remember when I was a young boy one day I said to him: "I am going to be a better preacher than you!" He said to me: "Oh I know you will, you are cheeky enough!"

They were both very good to me. My education was this; James lived in 15 Onslow Gardens and Gordon lived in 18 Onslow Gardens so I didn't know which house I was sleeping in that night. Those two men educated me, more than a seminary would. I learned the ropes of pastoral activity and I heard things that no one hears about and saw things that others didn't, so that was my training and it was the best training I could have had. In other words, I was supervised by the two of them. It's like in the Bible; 'Samuel served the Lord before Eli.' The Hebrew has it; 'He was *supervised* by Eli.'

I would recommend any young pastor to get in alongside your superior and drain him of all he has. Learn from him, spend time with him then go on and learn from others.

I remember Tommy Tenney (now international author and founder of the God Chasers network), I was close with his father. I remember him saying his father had lots of preachers in the house at night and they would have sat up late debating about things but he was told to go to bed. He came up with the idea he would stay up late to polish their shoes, so that when he was doing that he was able to hear all that was going on. That is where he got his best knowledge. It is very important to learn from the wisdom of others, especially spiritual fathers.

1 Corinthians 4:15; '*For though ye have ten thousand instructors in Christ, yet have ye not many fathers: for in Christ Jesus I have begotten you through the gospel.*'

In a dry land...

With such opposition against me moving to the Church of God I started to think that it wasn't worth going. I remember praying one day and I said to the Lord: "Lord I am not going to the Church of God, I am staying." But one thing I learned was delayed obedience is disobedience! This decision was the start of a dry season in my life.

How does it feel when God withdraws His touch from us? How does it affect our lives - do we even know the difference? For me, it felt like I was hacking at life with a blunt sword. The sharpness I had previously possessed had faded out. My prayer life had turned anaemic. The desire to pray was sucked out of me, and along with it went my discernment to hear the still quiet voice calling me to His place. At work the difference was noticeable to the office staff. No longer was I the bright and early riser who had already been up since dawn to pray, now I was a flustered boy rushing in just on time having overslept.

I knew this wasn't sustainable. I knew deep inside that this season would eventually reach a crescendo. The stubbornness had created a fortress around my heart that only repentance could break down, it was a question of how long would I wait?

For about three months I passed through this wilderness and I remember at work, I was nervous about lifts. One morning I made my way towards the Admiralty Office. I found myself alone in the lift and began the journey upward. I had always felt that lifts were precarious devices and better to be avoided, but it wasn't my dislike of lifts that was grasping my heart. Finally the loneliness and void within become too much. I punched the lift to a halt in mid-air and began to cry: "Father, what have I done? I need you!"

The barrier of stubbornness and resilience came down in a wash of tears, and there in that little box I heard the sound I had lost for far too long, the still small voice of the Father. "You have done nothing!" He rebuked me. I tried to rebuff the responsibility of my failure to the others, like Adam had done to Eve. I cried: "But Lord, nobody likes these people – they are heretics." But the Spirit's firm instruction remained. "Go!"

Stopped in the middle of these two floors I said: "Lord I yield to you." And when I did that, the anointing returned.

I exited the lift with a new-found resolve, the contest in the elevator proved the God whom I would serve, as I wholly surrendered myself to His will. I would go. I had to go. The previous months had been disastrous, I couldn't bear the thought that my disobedience would provoke even greater consequences if I rebelled a second time. The thought of losing that was far greater than the concern I had for what others would think. It was time for me to overcome. I bounded past the curious glances being thrown in my direction, I knew what they were thinking - what on earth was I doing in the lift? The answer? David was defeating Goliath!

These words should provoke a fearful concern for those who have likewise been entrusted with similar Spirit-birthed instructions. The question we all have to ask is, what will happen if I do not obey? For me - I can now see the footsteps through the dark and unknown places that led directly to what God had done in Whitewell. What if I had deviated and compromised on one little thing? Would I have come to this place today? Would I have been entrusted with the responsibilities God has given me? Or would there have been another, more humbled, more willing, more obedient Servant of God on this island or from another, whom He would have chosen?

The Scriptures are strewn with stories of men and women of God whose journeys led them through such situations. Some, like Moses, began by trying to carve their own way through God's landscape. Moses was humbled through forty hard years in the wilderness, and was restored to the call placed upon His life. Many however, like Saul or arguably King Asa, were not to be fully restored.

There is one thing we must always remember when we discuss the topic of obedience. God is not an Egyptian task-driver. He did not remove His people from the slavery of Egypt in order to tie them into forced and armage servitude. His yoke is easy and His burden is light (Matthew 11:30).

Even when I was working there in the drawing office, I would have missed some days as I was at Ormeau Park seeking the Lord. I just didn't turn up to work. Management knew rightly that's where I was. I got away with a lot as the staff were all wonderful to me.

When the time came for me to leave my boss asked me: "Why do you have to go? How much are you getting paid?"

I said: "I don't know."

You don't know and you're going?" He replied, puzzled.

I said to him: "Well, the Bible says Abraham went out and he didn't know where he was going."

My boss said: "Ach, don't be talking like that to me. Look we want to train you in the drawing office, to be the clerk of all the offices - a job for life."

I said: "No, I am going and the Lord is leading me."

He just said to me: "Look, we will give you more money - we will help you. I'll tell you what, I'll make a deal with you. Any convention you are going to speak at, I will release you to do that, you can go. You don't have to ask permission, as long as you come back."

I said: "No, I have to do what the Lord wants me to do."

The call was so strong - I just knew I had to answer it.

Chapter Seven

CRYING LIKE A BABY

After attending the Church of God for several years, I was approached by Gordon Magee who encouraged me to go to the North of England as a *pulpit supply*, for a minister who was taking a prolonged trip to the USA. With the benefit of hindsight I am able to recognise how this was just another stage of preparation for the future work God had planned for me.

The church was in Gateshead. I was told there was a congregation of twenty people and a widow who attended had offered to 'put me up' for my time there. I was only seventeen and was 'champing at the bit' to get out and serve the Lord so I agreed and off I went.

I got on the boat and sailed from Larne to Stranraer and then got a train down to Newcastle, just me and my two suitcases. I found 25 Deans Street and the widow lady who was keeping me wasn't in. She had gone out and had just left the key in the latch. I was so disappointed that there was no welcome. I remember setting my two cases down on her doorstep and bursting into tears. I cried my eyes out! Here was the great preacher crying like a baby! I was so lonely, there was nobody there, I didn't know where I was. I was just a boy.

But hope had its way. I was just starting out in the ministry, eager, and with a great opportunity at hand. My resolve in Christ wasn't to be compromised. Determined, over those next few months I tramped around the streets of Newcastle and Gateshead, visiting any open door and testifying to any open ear I could find, trying my best to craft true Holy Ghost inspired messages for the listening hearts.

Resources however were limited at the best of times, to say the least! The minister who had requested me for *pulpit supply* had said that a fair salary of 7 pounds 10 shillings per week would be provided, by 1955 standards this was very reasonable! However weeks went by and I never saw a penny of it, and the dear little widow was neglected of the 3 pounds most weeks for taking care of me.

A little divine inspiration came one day when the cupboards were really low. She remembered there were some lemonade bottles to be returned, so she dashed around to the shop, and cashed them in to buy our groceries. Those were the days of tough sustenance, but thankfully I had enough wit to realise that these tests of character were strengthening my love, faith, and dedication to our Lord Jesus.

As I mull over the memories of that time, I am compelled to remember the grace God bestowed upon the widow at Zarephath to sustain Elijah. Her unrelenting faith and obedience provided them both with oil and flour throughout the years of famine. It isn't an accident of course that Zarephath means 'Smelting' - the place where metals are refined. This little lady, whether conscious of her role or not, was the very means of God's sustenance during those months of refinement.

The next nine months were fantastic, as I did more outreach, the meetings were packed! The people came from everywhere. Originally there were only twenty people at the church, but the numbers swelled to around 500. It was great and the people were lovely. I gathered around me a lot of young people, we had prayer meetings and I taught them how to pray.

A specific night in October 1955 has been engraved upon my mind. Previously I had been spending a considerable amount of time walking the highways and byways of Newcastle and Gateshead, praying and crying out to God, petitioning Him that He might manifest His power and presence. I quite literally wept before Him on those streets, crying that He would move by the power of the Spirit.

My petitions were answered. I was standing alone in the vestry of the church after having a time of prayer with my workers. I could hear the loud murmur of people talking as the service began. As I left the room, pulling the door shut behind me, I was alerted to the presence of a row of Methodist and Anglicans - otherwise known as 'not Pentecostal orientated!' As I stepped onto the platform, a meticulously dressed lady fell down on to her face, mimicked by her two daughters. It alerted me initially as I have always maintained a standard of order and respect. Without facilitating a show, I quickly made my way to find out what had happened.

I was suddenly surrounded by the hushed exclamations of those standing around: "Vicar, did you see him?" I had been known as 'The Young Vicar' in those days, some even referred to me as 'The Young Father!'

"Who?" I asked. One person relayed the story with breathless astonishment: "When you came into the pulpit we saw a shining figure in a long white coat with bare feet, walking up the steps before you!"

The congregation saw him first before I caught sight of him. I saw he was wearing a linen ephod (a sleeveless garment), and he was in his bare feet. His hair was golden and he had a girdle around him. The people just fell straight to the floor. These days people are falling down under the power of God, but others are catching them.

However, on this occasion, there was no one to catch these people - they fell right down on their faces. I was alarmed because they weren't even Pentecostals!

It was a wonderful move of God.

Apparently he remained throughout the opening hymn as well, testimony to our choral eloquence I hope! It was not to turn uneventful from then however. As I announced the first verse, I was forced to stop. I closed my eyes and the congregation waited in silence.

"You." I pointed to a young mother. She looked at me like the proverbial rabbit caught in the headlights. I nodded my head as I responded to the weight of the Holy Spirit's call. "You tried to commit suicide today, but a voice told you to come here because you would hear words that would guide you for the rest of your life, and for eternity."

The young woman let a scream out for mercy, this total stranger to Christ was saved right there and then. I looked out over the people. Many had gone to the ground like felled trees and were beginning to pick themselves up again.

"What happened?" People whispered to each other.

"We saw Him!" Some replied.

"Who?!" Others asked.

"The Master! He is in this place, and He is in you!"

All of these things were happening and I hadn't even started to preach yet!

A number of people witnessed the Lord on many occasions in the church, and they said he looked exactly like me and was the same height. This was a wonderful, fulfilling experience and the little widow I stayed with looked after me really well. However, after the angel of the Lord appeared, she would hurry home from the meetings and go straight to bed, leaving my supper on the table. She wouldn't even speak to me because she was scared of this supernatural presence of the Lord! People became saved night after night. She had never witnessed anything like it and she was afraid of what was happening.

Sadly, my time was up so I had to return home. I found it difficult to leave the people as they begged me to stay but I knew I had to go. During my visit the church had been filled beyond reckoning, we'd done everything we could to house the people, from installing more seats to renting a large auditorium. Crowds of people who couldn't be contained were coming to hear the Gospel. Men and women were coming to Christ - coal miners as rough inside as they were on the outside, drunkards and alcoholics, and even prostitutes. They were coming in *hungry* for the Spirit of God, and the Spirit of God worked His way through, changing them and sanctifying them. It was a great time and five hundred people gave their hearts to Christ in that church.

Washing the dishes...

When I returned from Gateshead, I transferred to the Shankill and became Pastor James Forsythe's assistant. I did most of the preaching and most of the home visitation.

I remember James Forsythe and Gordon Magee both came to see me and they told me that a group of people had gathered at Whitewell Road in Greencastle. They asked me if I would like to go and look after them.

There were only ten people.

I had other engagements as I was booked to travel to Sweden, Finland, Canada and the United States. The world was my oyster right now and I didn't feel it was appropriate for me to pull out.

"Down to ten people?" I asked. "Ach, sure why don't you get somebody else?"

They agreed and I remember Gordon wasn't too happy with me. At that time I was staying up in Onslow Gardens with Pastor Forsythe. He was a little put out by my refusal so he scolded me and told me to 'go and wash the dishes!'

I did as I was told and it was there that God, the Holy Ghost convicted me. I never had an experience like it.

I was like a true sinner getting right with God. I was never in sin. I could never say I did this and I did that. I came to the Lord when I was a boy but I remember feeling really convicted at that moment, and in the middle of washing the dishes, I knelt down at the sink and said: "Lord I'll go there!"

So they came back about three hours later and I said: "Look, I have to go to Whitewell."

But they gave me the news that my decision was too late and that I couldn't because another pastor had been put in place.

I said: "Tell him he is not to go or I'll tell him!"

Gordon replied: "I'll tell him."

And that is how I went to Whitewell.

I will never forget the conviction at the sink as it was like what Abraham had - a horror of darkness came over him. That is actually what happened to me! I was really convicted because of my disobedience. I was 'the boy preacher' and wanted to be famous, I didn't want to be stuck in Whitewell with ten people! But the Lord had his own plan for me and I think he wanted to humble me, he wanted me to be a nobody. The conviction was really strong. I apologised to the Lord and I told him I would look after these people for the rest of my life. It really terrified me. My heart raced. James and Gordon saw how sincere and how honest I was and they let me go.

Unwillingness to surrender...

Going to North Belfast was never my first decision. I had visions of trail-blazing and touring all over the place, doing great things for God, all of my own accord of course. When I first heard mention of the suggestion to go to North Belfast my initial response was to shrug it off. Why should I have bothered pioneering petty work with a handful of poorly resourced believers? But I couldn't shrug off the concern of the Holy Spirit, the slight feeling that *He* had an interest in North Belfast. Once again I deadened the touch of the Holy Spirit through my unwillingness to yield.

I managed to convince myself that it was just a bad patch, a *lean-spell* as ministers called it, that time we all go through when our prayers roll down dry lips, and fall onto barren land. After all, the heart is deceitful above all things! How easily we cover over our footprints as we walk away from the mission at hand, destroying all evidence of the tampering selfishness. Most of the time we're not even aware of what we're doing. We are perpetually prone to disobedience, and continually vulnerable to absolving ourselves of responsibility. When we're challenged to step out into something slightly unfamiliar or uncomfortable, we strop in the corner like sulking children. It takes the light of the Holy Spirit to reveal the truth to us and to soften our hearts to return again to the Father.

I have always maintained that it is wise to keep short accounts with God. It is hard enough for us to return with all our fortresses of disobedience and rebellion, our fleshy human nature, never mind trying to return with a whole bag full of problems. Imagine returning a single item stolen from a shop, versus a whole trolley load.

The day came when I was determined to settle my accounts, I had felt for long enough that something was creating a barrier between us. I locked myself indoors and refused to leave for calls. If I had been slightly more technical I would have disabled the doorbell too. There in my room, face humbly resting on the floor, I affirmed to myself that *I truly do love the Lord Jesus with all of my heart.* Not knowing what else to say, I asked a simple question: "What is it Lord?"

His truth came flooding in like water through a broken dam. His light revealed all of the monsters hidden within the darkness. My selfishly propelled attitude and ambitions lay naked before my eyes, enthroned in my mind and dictating my actions before the

True King! It was the voice of pride-ridden self that had so casually dismissed the simple idea of going to North Belfast. I knew right away that self had to be dethroned, and that I had to go. Make no mistakes, I was under no impression that things were going to be easy. But I knew I had to be obedient and go.

One thing was for certain, I wasn't to remain the boy preacher for much longer. I was becoming a man, and that entailed a whole new level of responsibility before God. As a result, the life of David was revealed before my eyes. I remember the words of Eliab when David went to the valley of Elah with food for his brothers; *'With whom hast thou left those few sheep in the wilderness?'* 1 Samuel 17:28. He boy David was to become king some day, he had to learn the lessons of responsibility that all men must grapple with. I understood that like David, those lessons would be learned in the wilderness.

God's heart is eternally concerned for the welfare of His sheep. Sheep by their very nature are in need of care. They wander into bushes, get tangled in thorns, and fall into pits. It takes a person to truly love them in order to care for them, and that requires watching over the ewes with their young lambs, listening to their cries and bleats, rescuing them when they're lost, and sometimes even picking them up upon your shoulders to carry them. My Father loves His sheep, and that is where I had to be if I was to continue our relationship - If I loved Him, then I would love His.

Thankfully, His work is more than sufficient for preparing us, as he did to me - chopping, changing, pruning and weeding. Each conviction of the Holy Ghost was another victory leading me towards the actions that would save the souls of thousands of His people.

The first service...

It was the 23rd February, 1957. I awoke to see a drift of snow that had fallen overnight, the streets outside glistened with tender flakes. It was still early and the sun had not come up yet. North Belfast sat darkened under the shadow of the snow-covered Cavehill. Today would be our first service.

I made my way carefully towards the rented hall. Opening the door I was overcome by the smell of beer and stale cigarette smoke. I got busy with a fellow worker, Charles Purse, cleaning out the debris of ashes and cigarette butts, binning the leftover bottles, and mopping up a few precarious looking stains left on the floor, our hands turning blue from the frozen air. Ten people were committed, with another twelve visitors making an appearance. Twenty-two people. I stood at the front telling them about the great and wondrous things God was going to do in Whitewell. The service was set on its way. In the midst of the cold air, we were warmed together by the reading of the Scriptures and the breaking of bread. Suddenly a prophecy was declared, as we sat and silently listened, weighing up what was being said, and writing it down.

"Thus saith the Lord, you will remember this day. This day is the beginning of months, months of tears, hardship and difficulties. But if you will be faithful I will breathe upon you by my Spirit and give you a people that will touch this land. This church will become a reaping church and will benefit the community so much, the people in this ark will build a memorial unto you for my glory and honour. I will bring into your midst hundreds of young people and many visitors will come to you by aeroplane and ship to see what the Lord has accomplished among you."

I sat in stillness, trying to absorb the words that had just been shared, trying to discern how much, if any, was to be heeded. I tried to logically evaluate how on earth was this group of people to achieve these things?

Everything is to be judged by what it produces, prophecy more than anything. Scripture commands that prophecy is to be judged and tested, and well, the only way to do that sometimes is to wait and see if it will actually come to pass. The prophecy came with a condition attached, to be faithful, so at least then we had something to work with. But not everything comes to pass as quickly as we think it will. It's very easy to grow disillusioned and begin to throw away such promises. It took many years for these words to come to pass, and even to this day, it continues to be revealed.

Patience is required if we are to faithfully endure the months of tears, hardships and difficulties. Things often go slowly yet surely, and usually painstakingly. Conceiving such a promise requires a time of growth, and then there is the laborious birthing of the men and women He has chosen for this purpose.

Thinking about it leaves me in awe. Speaking of birthing, many of the people who were to be brought to Whitewell were not even born yet! Others yet lived great distances away, the name and place of Whitewell nothing more than a point on a map, if even that. Yet over the next thirty years, God was fashioning a people from all backgrounds - Protestant, Catholic, young and old, man and woman, all being born and born again, saved and matured, developed and grown.

And somehow, by God's divine hand, He would cause them all to come together, like the strands of a tapestry, to make Whitewell as it is today. Meanwhile, I contented myself with the little flock that had been stewarded to me, and prepared ourselves for what was to come, reminding ourselves of what the prophet Habakkuk said; *'For the vision is yet for an appointed time, but at the end it shall speak, and not lie: though it tarry, wait for it; because it will surely come, it will not tarry.'* Habakkuk 2:3

It was this verse that we kept in mind as we set about the work we had to do. As Paul wrote to Timothy in I Timothy 1:18; The prophecies would come!

Chapter Eight

THE McCONNELLS

Let me share about my lovely wife Margaret. It was in the Church of God in 1957 that I first laid eyes on this good-looking young woman. Because I was so full of myself at that time I just went over to her and asked her out – thankfully she said "Yes!"

They say, 'Love conquers all,' but a little money does help! When we started dating I knew if she agreed to marry me, it wouldn't be for my money! It is hard to impress a woman when you have no money so I told her I loved walking – my way of impressing without spending! We used to just meet up and go for long walks and that is how we got to know each other.

I am happy and deeply honoured to say that we got married in 1959 in the Orange Hall that we were renting for the church services when I was 22 years old.

The trial of hardship and limited resources didn't end then, but now I had a help mate. Together we laboured to make our little church strong and healthy. A man dedicated to God is not an easy man to live with, she not only endured the stress of reliance upon God, but graciously braved those years of living with a husband who ate, slept, and drank the work of God. She was an amazing woman who brimmed with patience and long-suffering that testified of her character.

My beloved two daughters Linda and Julie were born a few years after we married. Linda was born on 1st January 1961. I remember the day we brought her home from the hospital, she was so tiny. I ordered us a taxi and when we arrived at our home, the taxi man helped us out and said: "That's a lovely wee boy you got!" We didn't even care, we were so delighted to be parents.

A few years later, Julie arrived on 12th of July 1967. Margaret would always say that the Lord gave us those dates specifically as they were easy to remember. Especially Julie's, with her growing up in Northern Ireland! How wonderful that the country celebrates with her! As she was born on such a special date in July, we called her Julie. Julie is the rebel of the family but turned out a lovely rebel who really looks after me. I remember as a child she used to act up in church, she was so fed up and bored that she would ask her mum to take her out of the service to beat her! She would have made any excuse to get out but we persevered and took both girls to all the services.

We used to take the girls to all the meetings: early prayer meeting, late prayer meeting, Sunday morning service and the night service, mid-week meetings and monthly meetings – life for the kids of a pastor wasn't easy! Margaret and I had to carry Linda and Julie back and forward from our home in Kings Park to the meetings as we didn't own a car.

Julie's experience growing up was that she saw her dad criticised and saw her dad being treated badly and that put her off church a lot. As a young girl she attended all the meetings but when she came of age she pulled away. However I do know that she secretly listens to my sermons online! She is able to tell me all about them and also what is going on in the church. It appears that she knows more than me about Whitewell! She is married and has her own hairdressing business, so all the Whitewell ladies go in and see her and tell her all the news. If I want to know anything I ask Julie! She is very popular, everyone loves her. I am very close to both of my girls.

We were a close family but things were very difficult at times with the children as we had nothing. That was our main concern, that we had enough for the girls. We just scraped by, especially at Christmas. Life was hard then as I was just a young pastor trying to establish a small church but I was determined to carry on. We had no salary - we simply lived by faith. For thirteen years we lived on just thirty pounds per month. I didn't even own a car back then. They were difficult times and God tested me on many occasions.

The next George Best?

I remember at that time I was made a good offer to become a professional footballer. I loved football as a child. I preferred it to school and had totally lost interest in my lessons because of it. Our meetings were held in the Orange Hall on Mondays and Wednesdays. Fifteen young boys gave their lives to the Lord, but there wasn't much for them to do, because very few families had means of entertainment such as televisions.

I played football with the young boys on Tuesday, Thursday and Saturday nights. I wanted to help them stay out of trouble and by doing this, I unconsciously played myself back into fitness.

On one occasion, I went to the prayer meeting alone without Margaret. She was at home looking after the girls and there was a knock at the door. It was Jackie Milburn, a Newcastle United centre forward who also played for England. He was a football scout and had actually come to sign me to one of Northern Ireland's top football teams, Linfield. They chatted briefly but she told him that I wasn't home. I was flattered he wanted to sign me but I knew I had to be obedient to my calling.

There was another day I was chosen to play in a match at Ormeau Park and this man came over to me. I was goalkeeper; we used to just throw two coats down to act as makeshift goalposts.

He asked me if I played for anyone. I said I didn't and he couldn't understand why I hadn't been snapped up. His name was

Bob Bishop, the football scout who discovered George Best.

He said to me: "What are you doing?"

I said: "I came out for a time of prayer."

He said: "You what?"

He looked at me as if I was mad! He asked me would I sign up but I said no because I was pastoring a church and didn't have the time. He made it clear that he thought I was crazy! He obviously thought I had potential but I wasn't interested then, I just wanted to follow Christ. I didn't care how tight things were financially, I wasn't going to give up on the call that God had placed inside me to preach his Word.

It is at this test where many a man has succumbed to the enemy's offer to give up. The stretching or lack of resources was the first test of the Israelites in the wilderness. Their grumbling and complaints landed them a sentence of forty years wandering to purge them of their pride and self-entitlement. This proving and training can do no man any harm, in fact, it is essential that we are built up from the humbling little places. There is nothing wrong with being given the opportunity to honestly pray as I did - *'Give us this day our daily bread.'* (Matthew 6:11) Do not disqualify yourself as many men have. The sacrifices are worth it as we store up our treasures in heaven.

Looking back, it took thirteen years. That was the length of time we were married before going on holiday together with our two children. Another year later, we got our first car. Some pointed their fingers at us as if we were fools for putting the work of God and His people before ourselves. How can we judge if we were or weren't, but one thing is certain, we did it for the Lord, abiding in Him we bore fruit in the work.

I remember when the girls were young and I was writing my sermons, Margaret used to say to the them: "Now don't be running around the house when your dad is writing."

Of course as kids, they used to run in and out of the house anyway with friends and I would come out and shout at them.

"Away with you! Give my head peace - away you go!" I'd shout.

Then as the years went on I had to learn to close myself down to the noise around. The television could be on, people could be talking and I sat and wrote my sermons, not even hearing what was going on in the background. Closing down the background noise of your life will allow you to hear what God is saying now.

A very special moment...

I remember when Linda was eight, we had just moved to the Serpentine Road. One Sunday evening I was preaching in the Orange Hall and Linda realised she had to become saved.

That night I led Linda to the Lord, she usually took a wee colouring in page or something with her to church, but she forgot it that night so she just had to sit and listen.

I was preaching and she says that she just knew within herself that she had to develop a personal relationship with Christ. She needed to be saved - that was what was laid on her heart that night, so she decided it was time to get right with God.

Even at such a tender age, she knew it wasn't our responsibility to get her into Heaven – she had to make that choice herself and do it personally.

She waited until we got home. We were only in through the door and we were just taking our coats off when she said to me: "Daddy, I want to get saved."

Just beside the kitchen was a wee scullery. We didn't even have carpet on the floor. We had a wee settee that someone had given us, I remember it was orange. We knelt down beside the open fire in that room and we prayed together, just myself and Linda. I was thrilled and I know for a fact to this day, Linda has never looked back. It was the greatest moment of her life, coming to know the Lord as her own personal Saviour. And I know I was a huge influence in her life too. In fact, Linda came to work for the church in 1981, as an administrator.

Linda went on to meet her husband Norman who became a pastor in the church. I remember the day of her wedding, we pulled up outside the church and there were cars everywhere! I remember saying: "Look at the crowd today - I could lift a good offering here!"

So we had a wee laugh about that as we were getting out of the car. After the service, Norman and Linda got treated with a special guard of honour. Some of the men who were working on the church building at the time stood to each side of them with their spades, pitch forks and whatever was in their hands at the time! It was funny.

Confession, good for the soul...

Before I close this family part, let me return to my wife whom I met all those years ago and the lady who stood by me all these years - Margaret.

The Bible says; 'Let the weak say I am strong!' That was always a good verse for me to stand on when anyone would ask Margaret: "What would you say James was not the best at?" Without any hesitation, in fact, I don't even think she takes time to think, she would always say – "Handyman, he must be the worst one ever!"

Yes, when I look back, even though I was always happy to help out where I could, the fact was – I have done more damage than good! DIY is just not for me!

If we are able to become strong in our weak areas, then it is important to learn about our weakness.

My weakness, according to Margaret is my handyman skills, but according to me, it has to be my temper! Yes, I have confessed it, it is now out there! There have been different times throughout my life that my temper has taken over.

It's my John Wayne side, who was my favourite cowboy. Many will know he has Northern Irish roots as his ancestors came from County Antrim, Northern Ireland.

There were times when the John Wayne phenomenon shone through in my life. It happened the time the caretaker in our first rented hall was causing unrest and people were not only aware but also upset about it. It was an awkward situation for us to be in so I took the decision to sort it out. The man resented us being there. He pointed to a few crumbs on the floor and said: "Look at the mess your ladies left – Clean it!" Like a young boy I lifted a brush and cleaned the floor, then I closed the door – John Wayne had come out of me!

When I put the snib on the door, he asked me what I was doing. I just grabbed him, lifted him up and said: "One more word out of you and you're finished!" And I never experienced any trouble with him again because I'd hung him up like a coat-hanger!

I remember another day knocking two guys out, their bodies hitting the ground as they were stealing from the church. I believe in standing up for what I believe in, standing against corruption and injustice.

Before you start sending me in all your letters quoting Scripture, just remember, we all have a weakness. Yours may not be temper but it could be jealousy, pride, fornication, adultery, stealing, back-biting or dare I say it – gossip!

Each one of us has something that causes us to always be turning to our Lord and Saviour, Jesus Christ. We are but mere bone dressed in flesh depending on a God that graced us with His

Gospel of Salvation. He tells us in the book of Ephesians; *"It is not of works lest any man should boast."* No matter how hard I strive to be perfect, I realised years ago 'perfection' is only found in One and you and I are not Him – It is Jesus Christ our Lord.

You may ask: "Do I still have a temper?" The answer is yes, but do I still yield to it? That is the more important question.

At times from the deep caverns of my soul it seeks for the opportunity to break out and be itself – riotous! But I have come to realise through Scripture, Paul says in 1 Corinthians 15:31; *'I die daily!'* Note he did not say, I die weekly on a Sunday, or yearly on New Year's Day, but daily!

Each one of us needs the Living Christ dwelling within us and if He is within, whether we like it or not, sometimes He may want to change the furniture of the house that He dwells in and for that to happen we need to die daily!

When I hit my finger with a hammer, as Margaret is shouting: "You're going to miss the nail!" Am I tempted to enter the realm of temper? Yes! But do I now? No! Instead I realise it is but a season. That season might be for a minute while I am frothing with pain from my blackened nail or it could be a day or even a week where two spouses have stopped speaking. But whatever causes us to step over the line, to miss the mark, to fall short of His glory I am glad Scripture states in 1 Corinthians 10:13; *'There hath no temptation taken you but such as is common to man: but God is faithful, who will not suffer you to be tempted above that ye are able; but will with the temptation also make a way to escape, that ye may be able to bear it.'*

But when I ask Margaret what am I good at? Without any doubt she would say that when I am in the pulpit, I'm a master, but outside it, I'm a disaster! And that is the truth!

Even Linda would often say to me: "Daddy if you couldn't preach, I don't know what you would do."

Chapter Nine

AN AMAZING TESTIMONY

I was walking along Royal Avenue, just past the old C&A with three other ministers in the summer of 1960. It was the centre of Belfast and the schools were all off so the streets were really busy. Everyone was coming in and out of the different shops laden with shopping bags. We were just dandering along chatting away about the lovely day that it was. I was just about to speak to one of the other ministers when a lady I recognised caught my eye. She shouted to me from across the street.

"Jim McConnell?" It was a local lady and she was pregnant. She was a prostitute. I remember one of the ministers tutted and said: "Don't bother, just let her go."

I couldn't do that. I couldn't just ignore her and walk on, so I stopped and crossed the road to speak to her.

She said to me: "When I have my baby, would you dedicate the child?"

I said: "Yes, certainly, when you have your baby, just bring it down to the Orange Hall."

So, months later she gave birth to the child, and I dedicated it, despite the negativity from others.

She went on to give her heart to the Lord. This lady then told me that she wanted to help me.

So she took it upon herself to go around rapping doors and telling people: "I used to be a prostitute and I've changed my life around - I now go to Jim McConnell's church!"

I had to say to her: "For dear sake, don't tell people what you used to do and don't associate your profession with me!"

Having a good heart, she wanted to bring people through our doors, so one night she hired a double-decker bus, which was unheard of in the 1960s. She managed to pack it full of people.

The passengers were hanging out of the windows and standing in the aisles - it was like a mobile Bellevue Zoo. I couldn't believe my eyes when the bus load arrived and this lady was standing ushering them out and into the church to take their seats. She was quite a character!

She had a great personality. She hired the conductor and all. It packed out the church! I remember she used to go down to Merville Garden village and would tell all the old dears about Jesus and that she used to be a prostitute - they were horrified! Nobody knew what to make of her, but such a soul-winner for the Lord she became. She is now pastoring a church in England though many a time I think I could do with her back here. Filling a double decker bus and introducing people to Christ!

Thirteen years lost...

I spent thirteen years in the Orange Hall, trying to hold the church together and encourage it to grow and increase its membership. After the world had become my oyster, I now felt lost and insignificant.

Our congregation numbered sixty people.

We wanted to build a church properly, so we obtained a piece of land at the bottom of the Whitewell Road - it was on a hill and the Methodist Church was right beside it. The site was excavated but the works veered too close to the Methodist Church and the minister and congregation panicked – they thought the digging would have a detrimental impact on their foundations. They threatened to bring a court case against us and this caused a huge uproar between the two churches.

Our sixty people then panicked too and twenty of them left the church. That was a huge blow to lose virtually a third of the church.

We held on but were obliged to build a retaining wall, around 7ft tall, with reinforced concrete to hold up the Methodist Church. It cost us £2500 and it used up all our savings. In 1963 that was a lot of money. We persevered with saving until we collected enough money and eventually opened in 1969.

It was around that time that 'The Troubles' began and we bought our first bus and then purchased seven more. The *powers to be* in the Church of God objected to us having them. With the burning of the buses during the Belfast riots the leadership in the Church of God didn't want the people coming to church in them. They asked me to forget about the bus ministry. I wouldn't listen, my passion was to reach the lost and I didn't care how they got there – cars, buses or trains! The object was to get the people to hear the gospel. In the end, we had a total of 47 buses and later hired eight 52 seater buses. It got to the stage that I had to resign from the Church of God as they objected to the changes. Whitewell went independent and we had an association with the Elim church.

If we needed anything done I found out the way to make it happen was to get the women on your side, then the old men had to agree with their wives. When I left the Church of God, not one of my members went to them. I think the people saw I had something and so they followed me. I remember Gordon Magee saying to me, "Jim, I wouldn't doubt one word you said to me as I trust you." They never doubted what I had, they never doubted the anointing that was on my life.

The first thirteen years were fraught with difficulties. I kept seeking God and crying out to him. I was so frustrated. It broke my heart. I remember sitting on a wee stool in front of the fire in Serpentine Road reading the Saturday night Telegraph church notices.

One of the notices stated that Willie Mullan, a Baptist preacher who was a great friend of Rev Ian Paisley, held a Bible class on a Tuesday night. The notice pointed out that he planned to hold a class on the life of Daniel. Apparently around 600 attended these classes on a weekly-basis! I couldn't believe it, I was lucky if sixty people turned up on a Sunday night! I asked the Lord to place His hand on this situation because I was frustrated.

Men of God will always go through tough times, whether it is financial difficulty, lack of resources, or just sheer discouragement. Every man must carve his own path in the wilderness to receive his own anointing from God, and no anointing is the same. When I was faced with discouragement, I would retrace my steps from when I was a boy and relive the moment when the Angel of the Lord touched me. For a moment I would remember the awe that I experienced.

Faithfulness is the currency of God's work. If a man is faithful himself, faithful men will follow. Find out the will of God for your life and be faithful to what He has shown you. I feel that people have underestimated the faithfulness to the work of Whitewell. The loyalty and commitment that exists among the people is the result of a firm faithfulness to what God has called us as a family to do. The vision, that Whitewell is a lampstand to the people around the province, has sustained the older generation, and now we can see that same faithfulness filtering down to the younger generations of men and women. We are to be a witness to the nation, and the people know that. Anything else, and we are just playing church. Treating God's work as a hobby will get you nowhere.

Stormy seasons in our lives...

I remember walking down the Shore Road one day, it was raining and my feet were soaking. I had holes in my shoes and I hadn't any money to get on the bus. I prayed outside where Whitewell is now and I said: "Lord if it is your will for me to look after fifty to sixty people, I promise I will do it for the rest of my life and I will spoil them and look after them!"

During this season I was very discouraged, I felt like I was continually praying and nothing was happening. My prayers were repetitive but what kept me going was the passage in Matthew 7:7; *'Ask, and it will be given you; seek, and ye shall find; knock, and it shall be opened unto you.'*

The Greek new testament reads "Keep on asking!" Keep on Knocking, Keep on seeking."

I was one of those men who walked and prayed. Most mornings and evenings my feet could be heard pounding along the pavements of North Belfast, my mouth uttering fervent prayer that only a close observer could hear. It was my prayer life that sustained the work of God. During those hours I would communicate my heart to God, and He would communicate His heart to me. There in the waking or sleeping hours I would find rest and peace in His presence, and vision - vision to move forward.

It is nearly impossible to enter into that place of prayer with God, and not be provoked to change. Often it was during these times when God would alight what I thought were my concerns, but turned out to be convictions of truth, workings by the Holy Ghost.

I began to grow righteously frustrated with the systems around me; political hypocrisy - even amongst the churches, and the catholic hierarchy. There was a lack of vision for the nation among the political and religious leaders, and well, as the Scriptures state;

'*Where there is no vision, the people perish.*' Proverbs 29:18. While the Church steeped itself in hypocrisy - condemning the brutality, but offering little else, I spoke out against what I saw happening. How could we be spirit-filled and washed in the blood of Jesus, and yet be doing nothing for our land?

Well, a small price had to be paid for speaking the truth. Quite often I would be awoken late at night by the telephone ringing. I'd fumble around in the darkness trying to turn the light on, and then would make my way towards the call. The last thing I wanted to do was to avoid the call of a person in need. Occasionally it was something important, but sometimes I would hear the voices of men and women recounting the insidious threats of what they'd do if I didn't stop preaching.

When I was out praying one day I felt a wave of discontentment. Here I was, James the preacher-politician, the man with all the right things to say, reaping a minuscule persecution, but truthfully, impacting very little. I found myself pounding along the pavement, day after day, petitioning God to anoint me by His Spirit. Rain, hail, snow, I was there, trudging along. Even in the midst of trouble and danger.

Police Land Rovers and army vehicles would scream past me, grinding to a halt to expose who the young man wandering around in the pouring rain was. It came as a shock for them to see my prayer-filled face beaming at them as I handed them my identification and told them I was out praying. If it wasn't for my consistency they might have thought it was a good cover for suspicious activity. But regardless, I was there, sometimes having to get driven back home by concerned officers when things were getting a little too intense for their liking. I remember one night in particular, a young police officer called out to me from his armoured vehicle: "Are you finished yet?" There was great tension in the area and he wanted me home.

Carpet in, carpet out...

I was trusting for the harvest, I was believing something would happen. At that time in our home, we were surrounded by bare wooden floors. We didn't even have the luxury of a carpet on the stairs.

I remember a man from the church came to our home one day, the house was bare. He said: "I tell you what I am going to do, Pastor, I am going to carpet your stairs for you." So a couple of weeks later, a couple of men arrived in a van and carpeted the stairs.

A week later that same van arrived again and took it away. His wife had objected to this. We were just getting used to enjoying the carpet and suddenly it was gone, back to the bare boards.

It happened on another occasion too. I recall another man offering me his book case which was filled with reading material. He arrived at my door and said: "This is yours because you need them more than I do!" The next week his wife came and took them back! So it was obvious to me who wore the trousers in those houses!

You may ask, how did you feel when this happened? At first, we were embarrassed but afterwards we laughed at the thought of it. Later on, God would make our home beautiful. We learned not to rely on people, but Him alone. Lots of people promised us different things but nothing ever arrived. However, it was God who looked after us and blessed us. I was aware that God was testing me, to see what kind of person I was. I am a fighter even though I was an orphan.

We endured those hard times and we survived them as we believed that God had called us to do work. I knew nothing. I was just an orphaned boy who used to roam the streets. I didn't go to school. My school reports were appalling, so I didn't tell anyone about them. I just put them in the fire. With my dad in hospital and my grandparents elderly, they didn't realise. All I was ever interested in was football.

We were poor. I had holes in my shoes so Margaret used to cut out pieces of cardboard and put them inside, holding them down with tape just like insoles.

It was at the end of these thirteen years that we erected our first building which many will remember as the wee church with the spire at the bottom of the Whitewell Road.

It was a stark contrast to home, because we had very little. All my trust was in the Lord. I knew He would bring us through these difficult times. I recall singing a hymn written by Pastor Edward Mote of Rehoboth Baptist Church, England. In those days it was so true to me and to our situation...

My hope is built on nothing less than Jesus' blood and righteousness;
I dare not trust the sweetest frame, but wholly lean on Jesus' name.
On Christ, the solid Rock, I stand; all other ground is sinking sand.

When darkness veils His lovely face, I rest on His unchanging grace;
In every high and stormy gale, my anchor holds within the veil.
On Christ, the solid Rock, I stand; all other ground is sinking sand.

His oath, His covenant, and blood, support me in the whelming flood;
When every earthly prop gives way, He then is all my Hope and Stay.
On Christ, the solid Rock, I stand; all other ground is sinking sand.

When He shall come with trumpet sound, oh, may I then in Him be found,
Clothed in His righteousness alone, faultless to stand before the throne!
On Christ, the solid Rock, I stand; all other ground is sinking sand.

Edward Mote, 1863.

Chapter Ten

MAKING PROTESTANTS?

I felt led to go to Andersonstown to do a gospel mission. This is a Roman Catholic area in Belfast so therefore it was unheard of that a church like ours would enter this territory. Even some of my congregation were frightened to go but I was undeterred, to me they all needed saved! However, not everyone shared that view. A priest, Fr Patrick McCafferty who I'd befriended, opposed this move. This story made it on to Radio Ulster and it was also covered in the newspapers.

The leisure centre was earmarked for the rally, so we booked into it at Andersonstown, and this was received reasonably well by the residents.

The priest was unhappy, however, that I was going into West Belfast - he claimed that I believed the Pope is the Antichrist and that the church of Rome is not Christian! Fr McCafferty was the only one who publicly opposed it - the rest of the priests were quiet. They weren't happy, but they realised that it was freedom of speech and freedom of religion.

Even Sinn Fein President, Gerry Adams phoned me and requested me to meet him in Stormont. At that time I was Peter Robinson's chaplain; Peter was one of the founding members of the DUP. During our meeting together, Gerry looked at me intently and asked me: "What are you going to Andersonstown for?"

I said: "To get you saved and to get people saved!"

And he asked: "Is that to make them Protestant?"

I said: "No, it's to make people children of God."

I will never forget coming out of his office - The DUP representatives were staring at me and commenting upon my presence, wondering what I was doing with him!

That night the mission took place and almost 2000 people turned up. There were forty decisions. The leisure centre was packed, but some of our church members were reluctant to attend, because of where it was situated. All the television cameras were there too, so it was quite an occasion. I really enjoyed it – it was a very good mission. The people in that part of the city were lovely.

During the mission, a woman's home was broken into and her savings were stolen. I think it was around £3,000 was taken, so I told those present that we weren't going to keep the proceeds of the offering, but instead the money would go to replace the cash that the lady lost. She was delighted.

The big man and me...

I always seemed to be rubbing shoulders with controversial characters especially here in Northern Ireland. Many have said that the late Rev Ian Paisley and myself have been the voice of the Gospel in Northern Ireland over the years, but let me tell you how I met the big man.

I first encountered the late Rev Paisley as a boy. I used to sing and one night in the Ulster Hall he made me get up in front of everybody and sing without music and accompaniment.

Billy and Lilly Towel from the Bible Pattern Church wanted to hear an evangelist called John Wesley White, so they took me along and Paisley was leading the meeting. He spotted me in the crowd. I was just a wee boy at the time and I used to sing the odd solo.

He said: “Jim McConnell, come on up here and sing!”

So I took to the stage and sang ‘Come thou fount of every blessing’ without music. I was standing on the stage in front of everyone and it was going fairly well - until I forgot the second verse! I stammered: “I can’t mind the second verse!” The crowd exploded with laughter and broke into applause.

Little did I know then, that was just the start of me standing on stage in front of large crowds. I wouldn’t have believed then that I would return to the Ulster Hall as a preacher and would pack it eight times. I’ve filled the King’s Hall eight times, the Odyssey twice and football stadiums too.

I remember meeting Rev Paisley some years ago in Heathrow airport at gate 49. I was about to fly out to Spain, as we had work lined up there and I remember saying to my friend Jim Penny that I felt there was something wrong at home.

I was proved right when I heard the voice over the intercom calling me: “Would Pastor McConnell come to the phone please?”

It was Margaret. She broke the news to me that my sister had died. Jim flew out while I made arrangements to go home.

I was sitting at the gate contemplating the news when this tall figure approached me. He leaned over me and he said: “What are you doing here, McConnell?”

I said: “My sister has died, brother Paisley. She was saved.”

He said: “Thank God, you have nothing to worry about then.” And he stayed with me the whole time.

As Rev Paisley and I waited to board the flight back to Belfast, fog started to develop which meant we couldn’t return home that night. We ended up sleeping in the same room. In one sense, he stayed closed to me that night and yet every so often Rev Paisley, being the character he was, and me being me, would have a go at each other. But I have to say we always had the utmost respect for each other. I laugh when I look back now because we fought all night! Scriptural combat is what it is called. He saw Scripture one way; I saw it another!

I knew Margaret looked shocked when she saw Rev Paisley and I at the gates of Aldergrove, leaving together.

During my ministry in Whitewell, I received total support for the work I did - if any controversy reared its head, I killed it off. If anyone didn't agree with me, I just asked them to find somewhere else, I wasn't going to change. I was responsible for God's plan.

I simply told them: "There are five hundred churches out there - take your pick - but don't be coming here."

Some notable people did turn up at our church.

One night in 1987, I saw eight police armoured land rovers approaching the church. I was initially worried, thinking it was perhaps a bomb scare, but little did I know they were coming to Whitewell because The Rt. Hon. Sir Maurice Gibson, the Lord Justice of Appeal in Northern Ireland wanted to attend.

With him being the top judge in the country at the time, numerous attempts had been made on his life by terrorists, and at that time, the police were providing security for him. He gave his heart to the Lord that night. Sadly, six months later, the judge and his wife, Lady Cecily Gibson, were blown up by an IRA roadside bomb near Newry.

Chapter Eleven

MAN IN THE GALLERY

That day we opened the church was a most wonderful occasion. We saw a bit of an increase from 60 to 130 people, but still I wasn't happy.

I was frustrated because I knew what God could do and it simply wasn't happening. I kept praying; I kept seeking the Lord. I insisted upon disappearing to places where nobody would see me praying.

After my meetings on Monday and Wednesday nights, I would walk from the Serpentine Road, down York Street, York Park, and past Carlisle Circus and home again. I was seeking the Lord, asking Him to help me. I was getting frustrated too, because when I was praying in the church, people would rap the door.

So, I ended up having to drive up to Greymount which was at the back of the church, and I asked a few of the neighbours if I could park my car outside their door and use their garden to access the back door of the church so nobody would see me.

I'd jump over the wall, and make my way through the garden and into the back of the church.

One Wednesday I entered the church through the back and I

was up in the wee gallery praying when the man appeared again beside me.

"What is it Sir?" I asked.

He said: "Look this way - from this day I am going to increase you. Be faithful and from this day I will bless you."

Inside six weeks we went from 160 people to 600 people! That was with no forms of advertising, no nothing. The people just came. It's similar to what is said in Numbers 23:20 - *'You have given commandment to bless me.'*

That is exactly what happened. We began to grow and as a result the wee gallery was removed, we increased to a further seventy people, and a wall was knocked down. Part of the car park was also removed to allow for the expansion.

The church was packed to capacity inside a week! It was absolutely marvellous! An adjoining wall was knocked down to accommodate another 100 people.

The church continued to grow. On a Sunday night people were sitting in the porch and in the toilets - everywhere, so I knew another building was needed.

During the time of the increase, different people had different experiences in God. Margaret's friend Georgie, who was unsaved, heard a voice telling her to go to Whitewell Road one Sunday morning at 11am. Georgie didn't know God. She worked in security at the Castle Court. She listened to the voice and she became saved that morning. Then her husband came and he got saved too. He is still there, as a deacon in our church.

That was happening to so many people. There are a thousand stories like that where people were spoken to and directed to come. As the months went on and I got to know them, they would tell me how they came to be at Whitewell.

Winning souls...

I remember walking the roads, saying to the Lord: "Lord, give me a soul a week."

And he did just that. He answered my prayer. After the visitation on the wee gallery, I was promised the gift of the unsaved.

After that day, I was getting eighty decisions a night and at the rallies we held outside the church, I was having 200 decisions a night - some nights, 250.

From 1973 until today, every time I preach the gospel where there are unsaved souls present, they are saved because He tells me.

I remember the day I led my first soul to the Lord. He was a young boy of twelve who lived in Victor Street in East Belfast. I knew him because he went to Nettlefield School. I was praying in Spring Street one day and the Lord told me to go and see this boy. I knocked the door and spoke to him about Christ and he accepted Him that day as his Lord. He went on to became a church elder.

That day when the young boy yielded to Christ, it was a great encouragement to me. I can't even remember what I said to him, I think at the time I was speechless! There have been many times in my life when I have had no words, but as I opened my mouth the Lord filled it. I didn't realise then that he would be the first of thousands that I would lead to the Lord.

The man in the mirror...

Due to the church being packed out at that time we knew we would have to move. We established a piece of ground upon which we could build a larger church. The land was owned by Mr Agnew, a local businessman and it was to be sold to me for £35,000. That was a fortune in the late 1970s, so I basically told him to forget about it because it was far too expensive. Six months passed and I was in the back room knotting my tie in front of the mirror. Suddenly the man appeared to me again.

He said: "One of the owners is coming to see you tonight at six o'clock - offer him £15,000 for the land."

So I rang a pastor and I told him that the Lord had spoken to me and had indicated that I was to offer this man £15,000 for the ground. He developed a nervous cough. He thought I was crazy. Not only was that a lot less than they wanted for the land, but I didn't even have £15,000! I went out with one of my pastors and carried out some visitations, but I couldn't rest. I had to get home. So I sat the whole day waiting, and waiting. The six o'clock news came on and I thought I must have been dreaming.

Just then, the doorbell rang - it was a man.

I said to him: "I've been waiting on you!"

He said: "Did my secretary phone you?"

I said: "No, my secretary phoned me! I have been told to offer you £15,000."

"Who told you?" He asked.

I said: "I've already told you."

He said: "That's not enough."

He paused while he thought about it for a few minutes, then he said: "Wait a wee minute, could you give me an extra three foot of the ground right down from the pavement to the back of the site, so that my trucks can go down this way?"

I said: "Yes!"

He replied: "£15,000 - you are on!"

So that weekend at church, I informed the congregation that I was in trouble - that the Lord had ordered me to buy this ground, and that I didn't have the money. We organised a gift day for the following week and we lifted £18,000. We bought the ground and then started to build a church, initially seating 1,200 people.

Chapter Twelve

MEGA-CHURCH IN THE MAKING

The angel of the Lord manifests himself in a different way. When I worked in the drawing office, he came to me, and when I pastored my first church in Gateshead, Newcastle, he appeared to me there.

I began to seek God more and more. In 1973 when Whitewell was small and in its' infancy, and I was trying to build it up, the angel of the Lord appeared to me, giving me words of hope and comfort.

After that there was an explosion in the church, a sort of spiritual explosion. We grew and grew until we had around 3500 people at Whitewell.

God was filling every room in the building at that time. You wouldn't have been able to get to the toilet as someone was sitting on it listening to the service! At the time the church exploded, the BBC sent over Bernard Faulk, a reporter from London to find out what exactly was going on. It was chaos as so many people were trying to squeeze into the building and it was attracting a lot of media attention.

I was on The Kelly Show on television and various other shows. Gerry Kelly was amazed and told me that these people were coming to hear me speak.

I told him: "No, they are coming to hear about the Lord Jesus."

He argued that this wasn't right, that they were coming to hear me. I said: "Yes maybe, but they are hearing Christ's words through me."

A mega church wasn't initially the plan and it wasn't the desired route to follow. My desire for the church was simply for it to grow and to perform well. I never thought it would ever grow so large and swell in such numbers.

My passion was for winning souls. I was in a whirlwind. Every day, reporters contacted me by telephone asking me why the people were flocking to Whitewell. They were just trying to get to the bottom of the whole phenomenon. As the news of Whitewell spread, more and more people arrived to find out what was going on. I took part in a lot of interviews, but I will never forget the time I spent with Bernard Faulk. I remember him asking me a particular question.

"Do you steal sheep?" He asked.
I said: "No but I grow good grass!"

I laughed at the look on his face that day, but it was true. I wasn't interested in poaching people from other churches or other denominations, I just wanted them to know Christ and to grow in their faith. Bernard stayed for the church services while he was here to record the interview.

We had a stray cat that lived in the church at that time. He was lovely – a beautiful black cat. He came to all the meetings and was very faithful, watching all the services from under the piano stool. The Sunday night that Bernard came to visit the church, he was sitting on the chair and for some reason the cat scrabbed him on the backside! He let out a yell and it certainly made my night! Eventually one of the pastors adopted him – just in case he decided to attack anyone else!

Growing good grass is essential in a church - as there are preachers and then there are preachers. I always wanted to boast quality, not quantity, in my sermons. People need good food, you see. I recall hearing a story about a minister who claimed he could talk for an hour and think nothing of it.

The reply was: "And so could your congregation!"

During my ministry in Whitewell, I received total support for the work I did - if any controversy reared its head, I killed it off. If anyone didn't agree with me, I just asked them to find somewhere else, I wasn't going to change. I was responsible for God's plan.

I simply told them: "There are five hundred churches out there - take your pick - but don't be coming here."

Some churches have committees but I took the decision not to have one. Some pastors need a committee but I didn't. Some pastors need a committee because they are erratic - they need people to steady them. Thank God for faithful elders and deacons; they are Scriptural but sometimes in the movement of God's spirit, He raises a man. When God wanted Israel out of Egypt He didn't send a committee, He sent Moses and Aaron. In fact, two old lads. One eighty and one eighty-three.

It's time to get right...

Malcolm Duncan was saved in Whitewell. He is now a Pastor in Gold Hill Baptist Church in London and is a sought-after international conference speaker.

A few years ago he was standing outside the Robinson and Cleaver store in Royal Avenue and a voice spoke to him.

"Son, come home!" said the voice.

He tried to shake it off. His aunt, Mrs Hill started to attend

Whitewell and three months later, Malcolm ended up in our church, listening to me preaching. He literally sat on his hands during the appeal. And when he went to leave, I was standing there. I shouted to him: "Son, come home!"

He said it was the very same voice that spoke to him outside the shop, the very same sound, as if it was me standing outside that store speaking to him. It was the angel of the Lord and God's hand was on him.

That was what was going on at that time and God was drawing people in from near and far.

I remember a particular night in 1987, I saw eight police armoured land rovers approaching the church. I was initially worried, thinking it was perhaps a bomb scare, but little did I know they were coming to Whitewell because The Rt. Hon. Sir Maurice Gibson, the Lord Justice of Appeal in Northern Ireland wanted to attend.

With him being the top judge in the country at the time, numerous attempts had been made on his life by terrorists, and at that time, the police were providing security for him. He gave his heart to the Lord that night. Sadly, six months later, the judge and his wife Lady Cecily Gibson were blown up by an IRA roadside bomb near Newry.

Chapter Thirteen

TO THE ENDS OF THE EARTH

My pastoral years have brought me to almost every continent on the planet, from tropics to communist blocks, from large assemblies in grand churches in the United States of America, to humble gatherings in dirt-floored rooms in Africa. With so many opportunities abroad, often offering greater prospects of financial prosperity and security, and better weather, I'm often asked why I stayed glued to Whitewell.

Although many leaders come and go from holidays, enjoying the respite and rest that an excursion offers, for many years I can attest that I personally have never felt the desire to escape from the work God had placed me in. Even on our own holidays I would often be found on the phone to the church office making sure things were okay.

I travelled the world twice. The church exploded and I exploded all at the same time. I was out travelling around the globe. My first trip was to Indiana and that just ignited my desire to reach the world. One trip that sticks out in my mind was Columbia with my good friend "Drosty".

While I was in the Church of God, I fell in with a missionary called Bill Drost, who was an older man. He was a wonderful man, I loved him, we were very close. He was originally devolved from the Canadian army and he had heard of Smith Wigglesworth so he tracked him down. He knocked on Wigglesworth's door in Bradford on his way home. Wigglesworth said to him "Young man, you've got papers? You shouldn't be reading papers!" He talked to him and shortly he lay hands on him and prophesied over him, "You will go to South America and I will use you and bless you!"

So the years passed and in the 1950's, Drosty (That's what I called him), went to South America and for the first two years nothing happened. He was very friendly with Wynn Stairs, his missionary director. Wynn had heard me preach as a boy and he said to Drosty: "Is he for real?" and they studied me for two and a half years. I said to Wynn one day: "I know you are a man of God but who do you think you are? Studying me for that length of time, sure you are nothing!" I was angry that he was scrutinising me, he said he was watching me as he knew I had something.

Drosty told me that he went for a walk up a hill one day after he had written a letter to Wynn Stairs which said; "I am doing nothing, I am coming home and I will pay back all the money that you sent me for two years." As he walked back down that hill, the leaves were dropping off the trees and the leaves caught fire right in front of him and God said "Go you down there tonight!"

That night, twenty people were saved and filled with the Holy Ghost. In three months, he baptised 39,000! It was incredible! Then he retired, God spoke to him again and told him to go to Malaga. He hadn't a clue where it was, he looked it up on the map and realised it was in Spain. He rang me and said: "Young McConnell, you, your wife and kids come over to Malaga!" I took a mission for him and there were souls saved every night and baptised in the Holy Ghost.

That relationship between us built up, we had a kindred spirit. Any time he was in trouble he would ring me and ask: "Have you a few days?" I used to say: "Ach Bill, I have a few days but I have to do my work!" At that time it cost £300 to go to Spain, which was a lot. I had to borrow more £300's than you can shake a stick at! I was with him from Monday to Friday then came home to preach at Whitewell at the weekend. Everyone knew where I was, I was with my mate Drosty.

In 1976 he asked me: "Will you go to Colombia with me?" So I went and we had a great trip. Our lowest attendance there was 2,000 and that was at a prayer meeting. I had 3,000 decisions in ten days. Drosty interpreted, I don't know what he was saying but I carried on! The Holy Ghost was falling on them, we didn't have to lay hands on them, the Spirit was just at work. Falling in pockets, fifty people here and fifty people there, as we looked across the people we could see it.

After the last night, he said: "Are we ready to go home?" I looked at him and I said: "What's wrong with you?" He started: "I have a son in San Salvador..." I said: "That's okay, I will go with you!" He looked relieved and said: "Thank God, that is an answer to prayer, I didn't want to ask you." So we went and I will never forget it! The people were walking in their hundreds, carrying their chairs on their heads! I remember I was wearing a navy blue suit, a nice white shirt with a blue tie, I looked the part. Well, for a little while anyway. There was a dirt floor and when the Spirit fell, the people started to dance and jump and the dust rose! People were saved that night and filled with the Spirit. It was marvellous but I went home as black as my boot! I had to take my suit to the cleaners.

A few days later he said to me: "I have another son who lives in Panama Canal." So we travelled there together and were attacked by two men! Drosty took out a steel comb and they thought he had a knife. We beat the two of them and they ran! He was such a character! He was exceptional. They used to say about him, 'that he won more souls by accident than by design.' It broke my heart when he died.

Chapter Fourteen

CANCER COMES KNOCKING

We had a family crisis in 2000. I was lying one evening on the sofa and I thought of my daughter Linda and just burst into tears. I couldn't understand why I felt this way. I very rarely cry but I couldn't hold the tears back. I was in the house on my own and I knew something terrible was going to happen. I wasn't sure what was coming, but something just felt really wrong in my gut. I was restless so I took myself off to Ormeau Park for a full week. I walked the park, crying unto the Lord, calling out for Him to speak to me. I prayed and prayed because I knew something was wrong.

One Sunday, we were coming home together in the car and it was only myself and Linda. I hadn't mentioned anything about the feelings that I experienced, but I wanted to tell her.

So I revealed to her that the Lord told me that she was going to go through a great trial, but that she would come through it.

I could tell she was really astounded and she just looked at me with wide eyes.

About a month later, Linda first realised something wasn't quite right during our tent mission in Ormeau Park in August 2000. It was a Thursday night. She had come home and because it had been a hot, sticky night in the tent, she went upstairs to have a shower. As she was getting changed, she detected a lump on her breast.

Her husband Norman told her to make an emergency appointment with the doctor, and because she wanted to see a female, she had to wait until the following week, so that was quite an anxious period for her.

Linda was referred to a breast specialist and was given a Monday evening appointment. A mammogram was carried out and the results seemed fine. During an examination, the doctors didn't detect any abnormalities. Cancer behaves like that. I believe the disease is an alien, that cruelly hides itself and then returns.

Linda was then told she would have a scan and because there was some uncertainty there, a needle biopsy was required. She returned to see the consultant afterwards who broke the news to her that it was cancerous.

Linda says she felt she was having an out of body experience. She couldn't believe that this was happening to her.

After Linda got the news that Monday evening, she drove to our house and was sitting waiting on us coming home from the prayer meeting. When we pulled into the drive and saw her, we jumped out of the car and shouted: "What's wrong, what's wrong?"

Linda said: "Well I was at the Ulster Clinic tonight."

I said: "Yes, what happened?" and she blurted out: "Look, I have breast cancer!"

Margaret just fell apart and she broke into floods of tears. I was speechless. I just ushered Linda into the house. We all sat down and had a cup of tea. Margaret started fussing, telling Linda not to be going into work in the morning, and instead just rest up and take it easy. She wanted to wrap her up in cotton wool.

Eventually I said: "Linda, if you lie in your bed, you have cancer, if you get up and come into work, you still have cancer - so it's up to you love, what do you want to do?"

I was still in shock so I told Linda just to go on with her life as normal. She agreed with me and said she'd be in work as normal.

The consultant had explained to Linda that due to where the cancer was located, they could remove part of the breast, but this would leave her with some deformity. So she told him to go ahead and perform a complete mastectomy. The following Monday, Linda went in for the operation. It was very quick. Even though she had been delivered this huge shock, she still felt a peace and a calmness. There was no panic or hysteria. Neither of us questioned God, as we are His children and He loves us, so if things happen, I believe they happen for a reason.

Just because you are a Christian, doesn't mean you are going to go through life like a breeze. The Bible says that the sun shines on the evil and the good and the rain falls on the just and the unjust, so these things happen. I just believed the Lord was going to look after Linda so we as a family trusted Him that He would bring us through this.

So she carried on regardless of the cancer. It would prove to be a long road ahead as she had to begin chemotherapy. She told me that a woman's greatest fear is losing her hair and unfortunately it happened to her one Sunday morning when she was getting ready for church.

Apparently she got into the shower and she could feel the hair coming out. Then she started to dry it, and by now, it was falling out in clumps. She phoned her sister Julie, who is a hairdresser and asked her to give her a number one cut.

She said she couldn't handle it and wanted to be in control of the loss.

So Julie said she would open up the salon. Linda's daughter, our grandchild Rebecca who was only about eight at the time, went with her. Linda knew she had to stay strong for her and put on a brave face. Julie knew she was struggling, and I know it was hard for Julie to shave all of Linda's hair off.

It was hard for Rebecca to watch too.

Linda tried to make Rebecca laugh by telling her not to worry – that she would wake up in the morning and see two wee baldy heads in the bed and wouldn't know who was who! This made her laugh because her Daddy Norman was balding too.

Linda started chemotherapy in October 2000. She was very sick with the treatment. I remember Linda having her first chemotherapy and she was sitting the next day at home, feeling really sick. She heard a knock on the back door – it was me.

"Hello love," I said.
She was pleased to see me.
"Listen love, I just brought you a wee fish supper," I said.

Well as soon as the smell of the fish wafted around her, she dashed from the living room into the bathroom and she threw up quite violently.

So of course when Margaret heard about it, she said: "Och Jim, I told you! I told you!"

I replied: "Sure I was only trying to help, I thought she would enjoy a wee fish supper."

It was a hard time for everybody. Linda was one of the first of many women to have to endure cancer in Whitewell. I always preached that 'weeping shouldn't hinder worship.' That was always my wee line. So she attended all the meetings she could, even choir practice because she was a member at that time.

The doctors told Linda when she was receiving the

chemotherapy, not to be around crowds, due to the susceptibility to pick up infections, colds and flus. She went on to choir practice and everyone was coughing around her. Despite that, the whole time she was going through the treatment, she never developed one single cold. Nothing. I believe that was a miracle.

Even in the church office I depended on Linda, so this attack on her life had an impact on everyone. She continued working because she wanted to keep life as normal as possible for our family, especially her daughter.

Her prayer at that time was that she would still be around to raise her. She wanted to see her growing up and getting married. And thank God, He has answered our prayer – and Rebecca is getting married on June 1 next year. So He has been good to us – Linda is still with us, all these years on.

It's when something like this happens, you realise what you have inside to get you through. She always knew in her heart, that she was going to be healed.

I used to say to her: "Trust God every day. Those days will turn into weeks, and they'll turn into months, and they will turn into years."

I know Linda just trusted everyday and that is what happened.

Throughout the cancer we gave Linda as much support as we could. Margaret struggled a lot to come to terms with it. She tried to hide it from Linda, but she was very upset about it. Linda went on to have radiotherapy after that. Overall, it took about a year for her to recover from the cancer.

Linda like her mum, is a strong lady. She is also a great worker. Different pastors used to come into the Whitewell office and sit and watch her work to see how she did everything, then they would copy what she was doing. Linda is one of the best administrators in the country. Pastors used to come down pretending to see me but I wasn't there at all, I was out visiting.

It was terrible for the whole family but she was very strong through the whole crisis. Linda took everything in her stride. I often would say: "Linda was the best man I had!"

Chapter Fifteen

HOPE NO ONE IS WATCHING

I have been to the Holy Land eight times. Each time I have been there I have had a wonderful experience. My guide is called Dove, he was a tank commander in three wars and he was a member of their secret service. He has been with me on each trip and has told me everything that I wanted to know.

I recall one day, we were sitting in a restaurant after visiting Megiddo and we were chatting about Armageddon. The next thing I knew, all the chairs were shuffling around us and the people gathered. It was an impromptu sermon delivered there and then. I had an audience, I told them about the end of the age and how Christ was going to come and set up His Kingdom. So even though I have never officially been asked to preach in the Holy Land, I have shared with the people many times.

My guide always knew where to take me every morning, my first stop was always the Mount of Olives. He left the Mount of Olives to go into heaven and that is where He is returning to. It is a special place for me so I began every day there.

Everywhere we went, people knew Dove so I got testifying on our travels. We had many great experiences together. One time I visited when Hamas were firing rockets and I went by myself; Margaret was really worried about me but I went on. I went secretly, the church didn't know until the Monday night prayer meeting, they caught on I was away to Jerusalem. And when I came back, the following Sunday you couldn't get into Whitewell, it was packed! The minor hall, everywhere. They were crammed in to hear the stories about what happened. It was lovely. I called it the Samson syndrome. At that time, I asked Dove: "What's going to happen?"

He said: "If Iran act up, we will turn Iran into a glass car park."
I said: "A glass car park?"
He said: "You know what I mean!"

They discovered at the bottom of the red sea where Sodom and Gomorrah was, there was glass. When the angels destroyed Sodom and Gomorrah it was with atomic explosions. I asked him: "What happens if the rest of the world join in?"

He said: "We have 380 atomic bombs, we have one for every nation. We'll do a Samson act and we'll pull them down with ourselves."

I had lots of times of prayer in the Holy Land. I was surprised when I first visited the cave of Adullum. I often wondered how someone could hide in a cave but you could hide thousands there! It was powerful! The cave of Adullum must be twice or three times the size of a football ground. I would encourage anyone to visit the Holy Land, it really shows how accurate the Bible is.

I remember a few years ago, I did a teaching series with my friend Robert Gass in the Holy Land. It was powerful. We just sat discussing all the different regions and places mentioned in the Bible and their significance. It really is amazing to walk where He walked.

I was with Robert Gass one day and we were visiting the tomb. I would go to the tomb and the Mount of Olives every day so one day we went together.

That tomb is known as Gordon's Tomb. General Gordon never went to church but he always read the Bible. He was a great British General. He read that in the place where Jesus was crucified, there was a tomb.

I said to Robert: "I wonder what height the Lord was?"
He said: "I don't know?"
I told him: "You stand there and see if there is anyone coming."

So I jumped over the rail and I lay down where the Lord lay – I fitted perfectly! So we often laugh about that - that I am the same height as the Lord! We had great fun on our trips to the Holy Land. I am 5ft 6" on my passport, could it have been the Lord Jesus was 6ft tall?

I only lay in the tomb very briefly to make sure that nobody saw me but it was a powerful experience being there. There are things that strike me about where He lay. Firstly, the tomb was empty. The angel said; "He is not here for He has risen." You can visit the tomb of Buddha, or many others and see the inscription 'here lies' or 'the remains of so and so.' But when you go to the tomb of Jesus of Nazareth you will be told; "Why seek ye the living among the dead? He is not here for he is risen!"

The empty tomb for the past 2,000 years has been a difficulty to the critic and to the atheist for they cannot prove He is still dead! The empty tomb rigidly guarded by Roman soldiers proclaims; "He is alive!" So the angel said; "Come see the place where the Lord lay." The critic has tried to for centuries, the empty tomb frustrated him.

The second thing to note about the tomb is that, it was orderly. When they went in, there were the linen clothes lying and the napkin folded by itself! When the third day and hour arrived, our Lord awakening took those grave clothes off and set them neatly in order.

That morning for you and me, He took the sting out of death and robbed the grave of it's victory! He left the grave clothes for someone else. This was no desperate struggle or hasty victory. He did it as He said in John 2:19; *'Destroy this temple, and in three days I will raise it up'* Now it was the temple of His body.

And again, Psalm 16:10; *'For thou wilt not leave my soul in hell; neither wilt thou suffer thine Holy One to see corruption.'*

Tell me, if men had stolen the body would they have left the grave clothes behind? The grave clothes were very expensive!

And thirdly, it was also fragrant! He had left the grave, it was orderly and He left it fragrant. The spices the woman brought were still there!

It reminds me of a story I heard about a gardener. There was a musk rose growing in this garden for nine months, winter came and it died. The gardener was clearing up but he still could smell the musk rose, he couldn't understand it.

Picking up a piece of clay, he could smell the rose. He put his nose to the clay and inhaled its fragrance. The clay had been lying beside it all those months.

Some days after the resurrection a crippled man, lame from his mother's womb was healed by the power of the name of the living Jesus! This caused an uproar with the civil authorities. Peter and John were taken into custody and interrogated. Why? There was more to this miracle than met the eye.

Listen to Acts 4:13; *'Now when they saw the boldness of Peter and John, and perceived that they were unlearned and ignorant men, they marvelled; and they took knowledge of them, that they had been with Jesus.'*

They were like the clay beside the musk rose! They had been with Jesus night and day for three and a half years! They talked like Him, they acted like Him, they behaved like Him, they even looked like Him! Their demeanour gave them away but also gave to those who would try them and whip them, a flashback to Annas, Pilate and Herod. When they mocked Him, spat upon Him and crucified Him! He was alive in the hearts of Peter and John. They even smelled like Him!

Friend, that's the story of the empty tomb, that's the story of the Risen Lord! He's alive, He's real and He loves you! And He is coming again!

The harvest is white...

I was passing Finaghy on the outskirts of Belfast towards the end of January 1985, when I noticed a huge event was taking place at the King's Hall. The traffic was jammed; I had just reached the entrance of the King's Hall when the crawling speed ground to a halt. Young people were hopping off buses and running with excitement inside. There was a real buzz as I watched from behind the steering wheel.

It seemed to be packed to capacity, and as I was sitting watching the crowd, a voice inside asked me: "Could you fill it?"

Immediately I said: "No Lord, but you and I could together."

The Lord spoke to me and said: "Right we'll fill it together!"

My fingers tapped along the circumference of the steering wheel, the traffic began to disintegrate and I slowly made my way up to third gear. My mind ticked over with the words of Paul to the Corinthians; 'He that is joined to the Lord is one spirit.' While the Lord's instruction to me rang in my ears: "We'll fill it together!"

The Lord was true to his promise because on the first night, 10,000 people turned out.

I told the church that God had spoken to me about taking over the King's Hall, and they were all really curious. I could see all the faces staring at me.

I said to them: "Come on, let's reach the country!"

I arranged to see the manager of the King's Hall about making a booking for the event.

He said: "Aye, sure, what it is you want? Is it the thrupenny bit room you want?"

I said: "No, I want the hall."

He looked at me and said: "Okay, look we will give you the ground floor - that accommodates 6,000 people."

I said: "No, I don't want 6,000. I want the galleries, I want everything, I even want the statue removed at the back. I want it all!"

He said: "Young man, where are you going to get the people to fill that?"

I said: "How much is it? I'll give you the money."

We had a gift day, and £100,000 was collected. I will never forget that day.

On the morning of the mission, our church was broken into but thankfully there was nothing taken. The perpetrators must have thought the cash collected the Sunday before had been stored in it.

That night 6,000 people came along to begin with, and ten minutes later, more and more people started arriving. Unfortunately we had to start turning them away. It was unfortunate because we could have filled the King's Hall seven times over.

I booked it again for a weekend - Saturday night and Sunday night. We held a believers' meeting on the Saturday night and the ground floor was filled. We were pleased to get twenty-five decisions even though it was just a believers' meeting! Then the next night, it was 200 decisions.

That night I knew all denominations would be there so I preached on 'the middle wall of partition.' I pointed out that the Lord has broken down the middle wall of partition between us.

We tried to book the King's Hall again but it was unavailable for the date we wanted, and the manager said to me: "From now on, when you are booking this hall you are only getting 6,000 as we are not insured for 10,000 people!"

So we moved the venue to Windsor Park, and in the middle of that was the Bradford City fire disaster. As a result, all the stands at Windsor were also closed for safety reasons. We'd already paid the £20,000 for the hire of Windsor.

I was quite annoyed by this so I went to speak to management, but he said he couldn't do anything about it.

Our only answer was to borrow every chair we could get - so we ended up with five rows of chairs around each side of Windsor Park.

A total of 12,000 people showed up that night even though it had rained all day.

Our rallies spread around the city, and on two separate occasions we used the Odyssey Arena. We had to turn people away again, as we were at full capacity. Management pointed out that no more people could be admitted because of insurance problems.

Then we went to Clandeboye Park in Bangor, Seaview twice, The Oval and Ravenhill Rugby Ground.

When we held our tent missions or crusades in football stadiums and concert halls, we never knew who or what we'd be bringing in. We've had people from every political corner, with diverse religious backgrounds, even people with no religious backgrounds. With people comes all their problems too, problems that we pray are able to be sorted out to allow certain growth. But not everyone who comes is going to be good. Jesus' words captivate this reality for us in Matthew 13:47-48, '*Again, the kingdom of heaven is like unto a net, that was cast into the sea, and gathered of every kind: Which, when it was full, they drew to shore, and sat down, and gathered the good into vessels, but cast the bad away.*'

Only time can reveal the good hearts behind the toughened and scarred faces, the incredible wisdom that flows from the self-conscious and shy single mother, and the gifting in the hands of an ex-criminal. At the same time, the good faces can sometimes melt away and reveal a sinister heart. Supposedly 'together' people can reveal a myriad of dysfunction and brokenness that only time can reveal. It is our joy and responsibility to work with all kinds of people with all kinds of problems. What can be said of our call to the divorced, to single mothers, the fatherless, alcoholics, and ex-convicts? The parable of the hidden treasure from Matthew 13:44, ought to be mentioned; '*Again, the kingdom of heaven is like unto treasure hid in a field; the which when a man hath found, he hideth, and for joy thereof goeth and selleth all that he hath, and buyeth that field.*'

Working with people is about searching for their hidden treasure. You can't just go out and look for the gold and rubies and take them home, you have to buy the whole field and work it, clearing the weeds, digging up the rocks, and finally, hopefully, discovering the treasure that evidences the fact that they are a son of God, made in His very image.

Chapter Sixteen

ROMANIAN ORPHANAGE

Leaders are sometimes hard to come by and that's my honest opinion. There are other servants of God who have built up works, but all too often, they are mere men who are obsessed by money, men who love the office and men who want a vocation in life, and that's it. There's no fire inside them, nor any reaching out to those who need it the most.

Many of you will be familiar with the Romanian orphanage project which I was heavily involved in. However, it ended on a sour note, as that orphanage which we founded was torn down to prevent it falling into the hands of corrupt individuals.

It began in the year 2000, mainly because various people had come to Whitewell asking us to help improve the lives of orphans in Romania.

We bought a piece of land from Christians there, but were dealt a bit of a blow because they had apparently sold us the land for twice what it was worth!

Refusing to allow any setbacks, we sent out a team of twenty-five of our own men and hired a local worker to build the orphanage in a small village called Carani. The whole operation took three months, from start to finish.

Once finished, the orphanage was beautiful, aesthetically pleasing - it was just like a five-star hotel and it had the best of interiors. Indeed, many of the folks from Whitewell went over to visit the children from time to time, and they stayed in the orphanage with them.

The missionary's wife became a mother to those children, she was amazing with them. I thought the world of her.

But what started out as a dream project soon started to decay, when I realised something wasn't right.

I went over to visit the missionary and his wife. There was a Romanian guy working with us. He told me that these government officials wanted to see me so we had a meeting with them.

Five government representatives – four men and one woman - came to visit me and they were full of praise for our home. The meeting was held upstairs in the orphanage and they told me: "This is wonderful, this is just what we wanted."

However, I soon became suspicious when the officials asked my permission to place a child in the home for a month or at the most, three months at a time. I was astounded when I was offered $18,000 per child and I strongly believed that a paedophile ring was operating within the Romanian government.

"We will give you $18,000 per child," they said. "But we will come and take the child out when we want to," were their very words.

I believe if I had agreed to that, more children would have been held in the orphanage.
I questioned them.

"$18,000 per child? Are you serious?" I queried this, as we currently had fifty children in the orphanage, and the government wouldn't even give us $1 for those children!

I asked: "What is going on here?" and they wouldn't tell me, so I just said no.

They promised me money - but I knew I wouldn't have seen a penny of it.

From that day, the Romanian Officials were really opposed to our home and everything we were doing to help the children. I was absolutely disgusted because we were in a European country. We just didn't know why this had happened to us – it was almost as if it was a planned attack. It was very evident to me that this was a paedophile ring, and I wasn't going to permit it. I think they were frightened of me as I didn't give two hoots about them.

We continued on with our work, sending men out in teams to assist, until the building was fully maintained and thriving. The children there were lovely – such innocent and beautiful young people. I felt so sorry for them.

But I couldn't get those five government officials out of my head - they were absolute crooks. The woman was dressed just like a film star, but I told her and the other men directly - and I didn't hold back – I said they'd all be going to hell!

After the realisation that they knew we were on to them, they put us under immense pressure. It was just constant torment.

Then we received notification from the government that the children had to be returned.

I was furious, and felt there was no other answer but to destroy the building to stop it falling into the hands of paedophiles allegedly connected to the government.

Five men from Whitewell went back to Romania with me and we removed the roof. It was snowing at the time which was a blessing as the interior was completely ruined.

We smashed everything up, leaving a trail of destruction behind. We'd bought computers and other items for the home. All that was left was the bare shell of the building. Then we calmly drove to Hungary and boarded a flight home.

We had to do it in an underhand manner as we could easily have been jailed for a criminal offence. But everyone knows that Romania is just filled with corruption and bribery.

The poverty and ill treatment of children is sickening.

It hurt me, I felt terrible that this happened. When I brought the missionary back from Romania he asked me if he could join the staff in Whitewell, I reluctantly agreed out of pity for him but in the end, he left me anyway.

It's hard to get good men, it's hard to get consistent men. The Lord says; "Well done, good and faithful servant." But you can't be faithful without being good and you can't be good without being faithful! That's just the way it goes!

As a whole, Romania disappoints me. In my honest opinion, the bribery and corruption and often the poverty and ill treatment of children is worse there than in Africa. We have initiated projects in Kenya and Ethiopia, two of the most needy countries, but we never experienced any of the trouble we had in Romania.

Every single month, a problem raised its ugly head. A journalist representing a newspaper in Romania, wrote a negative article about our orphanage. The whole incident landed us in court, but we won our case. The newspaper was fined but apparently they didn't pay the fine - at least, that's what I heard anyway.

It turned out well in the end however, as UCB asked if they could have the orphanage and I signed it over to them. They repaired the damage that was done and are still using it today.

Following the inception of the orphanage project in Romania, there were two further works established in Kenya and Ethiopia. They are fantastic.

Helping the disadvantaged in Kenya...

I had the privilege of opening the Metropolitan Sanctuary for Sick Children in Nyeri, Kenya. The hospice is the only one of its kind, specialising in children. The medical clinic is staffed by two doctors who treat around 1,200 people each month. The young couple, Jason and Joleen Allen who went out and established the work in Kenya did so to help disadvantaged children. Many of these children suffer from illnesses including HIV, tuberculosis, cerebral palsy, rickets, jiggers and cases of sexual abuse. They also run a church.

Joleen who is an occupational therapist, developed a way to make chairs out of cardboard and maize flour. She can tailor them to each individual child, assisting them not only to improve their posture, but also making breathing easier. These chairs give the children freedom, enabling them to join their families outside where most of the activities like cooking are done. Several hundred of these chairs have been given out, all free of charge and there is a huge waiting list for more. The Sanctuary employ several mums of these children to make the chairs and also other paper products such as cards and Christmas decorations. These are sent back with team members to sell at home to help keep the work going.

The Sanctuary has been running now from 2007 when I had the privilege of opening it. I remember when we did so, we held a rally in a nearby slum with many receiving Christ. It was an amazing experience and many people have been helped through this outreach. This year to date, there have been over 6,000 children treated, receiving free medical care, physiotherapy, walking aids, spinal jackets, prosthetics, postural specialised chairs and standing frames.

Our goal with the Kenya work was that these poor and needy

people would be shown that they matter. This certainly has been accomplished as when you visit you can see that the love of God has reached this place.

Rapid growth in Ethiopia...

The work in Ethiopia is second to none. In the year 2005, James McClelland, a member of Whitewell congregation for over twenty years, felt a great burden for the land of Ethiopia which is one of the poorest countries in Africa. Without a word to his family, until the day before he booked his ticket to Addis Ababa, he went out not knowing what lay ahead of him. In the midst of thunder and lightening he arrived in a village called Kuriftu where he was led into a mud hut with no electricity. He believed God met him that night and showed him a plan to help the children and the people of Ethiopia.

At the same time a man named Bezabih Toloso who lived in the village Kuriftu, had been praying that God would speak to someone who could help his people. These two men, by the grace of God worked together to bring God's plan to fruition. In the same year, James visited the villages of Kuriftu and Babogaya. Here they were experiencing living conditions of extreme poverty, hardship and squalor. This was a heartbreaking experience for him. Life for the people and their children seemed so hopeless and without purpose. They needed help materially but greater than this they needed to know the truth of God's Word and that He alone can give them hope and eternal life through faith in the Lord Jesus Christ.

James and Bezibah, with the blessing and support of our congregation at Whitewell, purchased land and built a complex, some would say a village, consisting of a school for over 700 children who are educated free of charge, a clinic where children receive free medical care, feeding facilities where children are fed daily and each receive a free school uniform to ensure equality in dress for each child. Within the complex there is a 2,000 seater church where local people can come and be taught the word of God and receive the gospel of Jesus Christ, and a well with enough water to last for 25 years.

The Whitewell congregation, family, friends and sponsors have spent the last thirteen years building up the work in Ethiopia but sadly in January 2015, after many years of an uphill climb with illness, James went home to be with the Lord. Today in Ethiopia, God has blessed the village of Kuriftu and the work continues to grow. Many people say it is a mega missionary project and is still growing with a church and a school also in Babogaya which was completed in September 2016. In Babogaya, our second church plant not far from Kuriftu, 100 children attend Bible club twice a week. The church and classrooms have been completed and officially opened and we have enrolled our first 100 children. They also will be taught God's word, receive education and a nourishing meal daily.

Our third church plant in Ambo, a large town approximately a three-hour drive from Kuriftu is seeing steady growth. Within several months our congregation has grown to almost 500 and is in a temporary building. In July 2016, Pastor Bezabih and Pastor Lema, pastor of the Ambo church, secured 4,000 square metres of land to build a third church and school and we say; 'To God be the glory.'

I, another pastor and a team from the Tabernacle visited Ethiopia in February 2016. I preached God's word there to a packed congregation who attend weekly and many have come to Christ. This is the Lord's doing and marvellous in our eyes. Truly we can say of Ethiopia, our branches have gone over the wall.

Chapter Seventeen

COURTING FAITH

I was sitting at my desk one Tuesday morning, talking to some of my men in the church when the phone rang.

"Pastor McConnell?" A voice enquired. "Yes?" I replied.

"I am ringing from the BBC; did you say you don't trust Muslims?"

I was shocked by this question and wondered where this had suddenly come from.

I replied: "No, I did not!"

As the conversation continued the penny dropped. I had preached that previous Sunday night on Sharia law. I told him that I had no problem with Muslims, but I don't agree with their theology.

I said: "I am against their theology but I am not against them. I don't hate anybody. I wouldn't hurt a hair on their heads, but I feel their theology is devilish and is from the pit."

It was such a shock, completely out of the blue. I had spoken to the BBC before but never in this capacity.

Not long after the call I spoke to Stephen Nolan and he sounded so angry. Apparently, some Muslims had heard my sermon online and Dr Al-Wazzan, the leader of the Belfast Islamic centre had condemned it.

Over the next month, I appeared on the radio three times with him, live on air. I was in the papers for the next twenty-eight days. I was on television for a total of three hours.

I had preached that particular sermon some years back and I felt the Lord saying to me to look over the notes as he wanted me to take up that rein again.

I felt compelled to do so.

The text from which I derived the sermon was: '*There is one God and one mediator between God and man.*' 1 Timothy 2:5

I spoke about Muslims and their faith. On the previous occasion when I preached that sermon, there was not even a ripple of discord, but this time it sparked major controversy. I lost friendships through it, including two good friends who I loved.

The supposed controversy in the sermon was a result of my description of Islam which I described as 'heathen' and 'satanic' and 'a doctrine spawned in hell.'

In my sermon I also pointed out that I did not trust Muslims, but I was referring to those who practice Sharia law. I couldn't believe the trouble that was caused over five words of dialogue within a sermon and I couldn't understand it as I had preached many times before about Muslims.

The police came to see me and questioned me about what had been said. I told them that the whole thing had been taken too far and that they were trying to infuse into me political correctness.

I told them I felt it was a sinister move. I had a bad feeling about the whole situation. Just before I had spoken with the police, I was tipped off by a news reporter - he'd heard that there was someone out to destroy me. He tried to investigate it but all the doors were shut on him. I felt there was something sinister in this so I prayed about it and I said: "Lord I am taking my stand and I don't care what they do to me."

Some months later I was asked to attend Whiteabbey Police station. I was advised by friends to get a solicitor, so I hired Joe Rice and I couldn't commend him highly enough. He was absolutely brilliant and did a marvellous job. He sat with me the whole time in the police station. We were taken into an interview room there and everything I said was recorded. There were three police officers interviewing me.

It was like a full interrogation, but in fairness they were very good with me and I knew they were only doing their job. They didn't explain to me why I was there - they just started questioning me if I trusted Muslims. They talked about a crime of hatred. It made no sense to me. How could I hate Muslims when I am sending thousands of pounds every month to feed them in Africa? It was ludicrous, ridiculous. They kept me over two hours. Then they released me and I heard no more until a year later when they arrived at my home with a summons.

I knew they would be in contact again though as there was a storm brewing. I started receiving death threats. The police rang me one day at home and told me to be careful. The police officer told me to be wary of where I was going and what I was doing. In other words, he told me to watch my back.

Someone sent a package to the church for me. My secretary opened it and inside was a black rose with a note saying... 'your time will come!'

The police still have the rose today. I have never seen a black rose before. The church staff phoned the police immediately and they came and took it away. Following that I just kept my head down and continued preaching and it died down. Soon there were other news stories to report on and I was slowly fading out of the limelight.

A year later...

It was like any other Wednesday morning. I had gone to the church office early and worked till near lunchtime. I then decided to go home and have lunch with Margaret. She made us some tea and sandwiches and we were sitting in our lounge chatting when…

KNOCK, KNOCK, KNOCK - our front door was knocked forcefully.

I asked her: “Are we expecting visitors?”

Her reply was: “I don't think so!”

Setting my cup of tea and half-eaten sandwich down, I went to the door as fast as I could to see what was wrong.

I opened it and I was shocked to see two police officers standing there.

I invited them in and they said: “Mr McConnell, this is for you!” They handed me a summons and left.

I turned and came back in.

“Who was at the door?” Margaret asked me.

I said: “Only the police. It would seem I could be spending some time in prison.”

I sat down and enjoyed the last part of my sandwich and we continued to finish our conversation that had been interrupted.

I had to seek legal representation. I was charged under the Communications Act 2003. I was accused of improper use of a public electronic communications network, and causing a grossly offensive message to be sent by means of a public electronic communications network.

The summons was issued but no arrest was made. I was

threatened with six months' imprisonment. The court hearing was scheduled for a date two months from then. I was facing charges of inciting hatred and of severe discrimination.

This would be a trial and a test of my faith. I knew it was another chance to see God shine and another chance for us to grow in the Lord together - and this opportunity had just knocked on our door! We all like that 'pat on the back' and 'well done' approvals because it's part of our DNA. But instead of a 'pat on the back' it's the law of a country placing their hand on us and seeking to march us off to prison. Remarks on Islam were splashed all over the news, locally, nationally and internationally (I am sure you saw it). But the whole farce was NEVER truly about the Islam remarks.

You see, in the last days whether we like it or not, persecution will come, it will come knocking on our doors and we will then know if we are IN Christ or if we are just IN church. I learned a long time ago that my faith MUST alone be in Christ. He is the One who began the work in me and He is the One who is well able to finish it! You may wonder why Margaret and I continued on like nothing had happened that Sunday. In truth, nothing of great importance really happened to what is the most important part of us, our faith in the Master, Jesus Christ. A house has the ability to stand if the foundation is right against the storm.

A prison sentence was now looming, but at least I would have my three hot meals, my own bed, an allowance and a colour TV. The sadness is, this is nothing compared to the persecution the likes of our brothers and sisters suffer in other countries. We pray the prayer of salvation and go to church. They pray the prayer and their families are murdered, crucified on crosses, burnt alive so who am I to complain? Yes, I am an ageing man, a prison sentence was knocking and yes I was up for it. I was ready to pack my suitcase to go to prison, taking my books and my Bible with me. Church may not have been in Whitewell those coming Sundays, but I vowed I would do Church wherever I was. I felt the BBC, Nolan and many others sought to mar my name but they forgot that my name is hidden in Christ and so is yours if you are a believer.

Who is James McConnell? What is he? I am only dust breathed on by the Spirit of God and given grace to walk this path under God in life. I am a nobody made only into a somebody in Christ. I am no different than any of us who have been given an opportunity to come to know the Lord, but the key is - what we do with the opportunity, or as the Bible calls it – the seed.

The Bible says in Matthew 13:1-8;

'The same day went Jesus out of the house, and sat by the seaside. And great multitudes were gathered together unto him, so that he went into a ship, and sat; and the whole multitude stood on the shore. And he spake many things unto them in parables, saying, behold, a sower went forth to sow; and when he sowed, some seeds fell by the way side, and the fowls came and devoured them up: some fell upon stony places, where they had not much earth: and forthwith they sprung up, because they had no deepness of earth: and when the sun was up, they were scorched; and because they had no root, they withered away. And some fell among thorns; and the thorns sprung up, and choked them: but other fell into good ground, and brought forth fruit, some an hundredfold, some sixtyfold, some thirtyfold. Who hath ears to hear, let him hear.'

Did you read that? It was the same seed that was being sown… the problem is not the seed, the problem is the ground – you and me. How do I make myself good ground for good seed? Let me answer that from the Word of God...

Romans 12:1-3; *'I beseech you therefore, brethren, by the mercies of God, that ye present your bodies a living sacrifice, holy, acceptable unto God, which is your reasonable service. And be not conformed to this world: but be ye transformed by the renewing of your mind, that ye may prove what is that good, and acceptable, and perfect, will of God. For I say, through the grace given unto me, to every man that is among you, not to think of himself more highly than he ought to think; but to think soberly, according as God hath dealt to every man the measure of faith.'*

God has dealt to every man, you and I, a measure of faith! When something comes knocking on our door we must let 'faith' answer it, not James McConnell, but faith – that is how we pass the test. That day, as I answered that door, it was no different than the many other doors that I would have to answer in my life. But I knew 'faith in Christ' was the key.

After all, I am aware of some men who had gone before me or as the term is used *going down.* Let me name a few - Joseph, Samson, Jeremiah, Micaiah, Zedekiah, Daniel, John the Baptist, Peter, James, John, Silas, Paul, Epaphras, Aristarchus, Junia, and even Jesus himself, who was held in custody between his arrest and execution, and then, in death, was imprisoned in a guarded tomb. The least I could do is follow in their steps if God willed it.

Stand up, stand up for Jesus...

I was in court on seven occasions and each time the case was dismissed due to lack of information on their part. I was continually brought back, which showed the weakness of their argument.

There are people trying to appease other religions. However, I am not out to do that, I am here to preach Christ. I am not against other people practising their faith but I have a right to stand up for my own. Just as they have a right to stand up for theirs.

The media twisted my words and said I was against all Muslims. How could I be against all Muslims when I had Muslims attending my church? I had Muslims in my choir. I was also supporting Muslims in Kenya and Ethiopia financially and feeding them. Again, political correctness gone mad.

The police issued a warning to me, but I refused it. They told me I didn't understand what was going to happen to me but I refused to listen. I told them I had a right to free speech and I had a right to believe what I believe. I am not sure what the police wanted from me but I felt sorry for them. They had to investigate me because of what they had been told. They wanted me to submit, they wanted me to be a wee boy and I despised them. I despised them utterly. I took my stand for the Lord and I would continue to take it. And I would keep on preaching. What I couldn't understand was, I had preached sermons like this many times before and it was only this particular sermon that caused trouble. I think I have made worse statements than that, but still they took a sentence which lasted just seconds and they built a whole case out of it.

The priest who had lodged objections to the rally which I organised for West Belfast a few years previous, Fr Pat McCafferty, testified for me in court. As a result, he became a friend and a man respected by my family – even though he is different theologically. The West Belfast rally in my opinion was the greatest event I ever took part in – when one considers for the previous twenty years I had preached in different venues to hundreds of thousands. He had initially accused me of holding anti-Catholic views. He told them that I was honourable and I didn't hate anybody. He testified for me and East Antrim DUP Assemblyman Sammy Wilson did the same.

People travelled from London and Scotland to come to court to support me. I received over 20,000 letters from people all around the world. I was even interviewed by media outlets in America – all because of this.

I was due to appear at Laganside Magistrates Court from December 14th to 16th, 2015 to answer to the Public Prosecution Service for my remarks.

A year ago, I was accused of this 'hate' crime. I was given a so-called 'informed' warning but I refused to accept it because what I said I believed, and I believed it was right.

Under questioning by a defence barrister, I gave my reasons for refusing this lesser punishment. I said accepting it would leave me gagged.

I preached the sermon to highlight the injustice towards Christians in Sudan, specifically toward a young Sudanese Muslim woman, Meriam Ibrahim. She converted to Christianity and married a Christian man. Meriam was apparently given over to the authorities by one of her relatives, who claimed she was committing adultery by marrying Daniel Wani, a Christian. She was given three days to convert, but refused to, saying she had been a Christian all her life. Meriam was arrested during her second pregnancy and was set to receive one hundred lashes and the death penalty. She gave birth to her daughter, Maya, while she was imprisoned in Sudan.

Thankfully, after a long delay and a term of imprisonment, she was released on the order of a Sudanese appeal court. Meriam, her husband and family are now living in New Hampshire in the United States.

This was my main reason for preaching that sermon. Surely this so-called religion ought to be branded 'satanic?'

Who would do this to a young woman? In my opinion, mutilating thousands of women and imprisoning, torturing, crucifying and beheading thousands of men ought to be branded 'satanic!'

The Lord Jesus Christ who I serve would never do this to anyone! He is the Saviour of the world, who died on the cross of Calvary for us. During the trial, I appealed to Christians to support me in my stand for the truth. The Lord Jesus said in John 14:6; "*I am the Truth.*" I asked supporters to come to Laganside on 14th, 15th and 16th December to show the whole of the world that men and women refuse to be gagged for standing up for the Gospel of Jesus Christ.

I knew that Jesus was with me and I was confident that I would come out the other end and continue preaching the Gospel again.

I also appealed to Muslims and challenged them to come and support me.

"No-one is questioning your right to worship here and practice your religion. If I was living in many Muslim countries in the world, I would be forbidden to practice my religion and would probably be imprisoned or even put to death for doing so. Yet you, as a Muslim, have perfect liberty here. So I appeal to you, come with me and protest," I said.

I challenged people not to sit on the fence or in their *comfort zone* and compromise.

As a child I used to sing a hymn in Sunday School: '*Stand up, stand up for Jesus. Ye soldiers of the Cross!*' It was time to stand up and be counted!

Chapter Eighteen

THE RIGHT OF FREE SPEECH

During my appeal I knew it would be a test case for the days that lay ahead.

If the prosecution won, then they would succeed in curtailing every word preached from the pulpit and the very prayers prayed in Church. I was conscious that our beloved Northern Ireland would turn into a 'police state!'

I said, no matter what religion you are - whether you are a Muslim, Hindu, or Buddhist – you have a right to free speech and the right to worship in the way you have been taught.

I may disagree with what you believe in, but I will fight for your democratic rights to say it and practice it.

I was aware of the hidden and sinister powers at work in this country, and therefore I asked people to come out and protest.

I knew that if I went to prison it would be a travesty of justice. And I knew that after my imprisonment when I was released, I would come out and do it all over again.

John Bunyan, the English writer and author of Pilgrim's

Progress was imprisoned for preaching the gospel and, when he was released, he returned to serving God - and back again he went to jail! During his second sentence, he wrote the book.

With this in mind, I asked for the people of Ireland, North and South, to make the 14th, 15th and 16th December red-letter days - and to put Christ first in their lives.

I was adamant that if the judge fined me, I would not pay it, and I told the congregation in the church that nobody was to pay the fine for me. I told them it was a matter of principle.

I knew that paying a fine would be an admission of guilt and I was an innocent man. I knew at the time that refusing a fine could mean imprisonment, but I was prepared.

I imagined life in prison. I planned to pack all my belongings and use my time to minister to the inmates. I was always willing to go to jail for my beliefs.

I felt like Peter and John when the Sanhedrin forbade them to speak or teach in the name of Jesus. Their reply; '*For we cannot but speak the things which we have seen and heard.*' Acts 4:20.

The entire case took eighteen months from beginning to end.

The trial lasted three days and took place in December. The verdict was delivered almost a month later, on 4th Jan 2016.

On the day of the verdict, I broke out in shingles. I wasn't nervous and I didn't have one sleepless night during the court process, but subconsciously I must have been under strain. I was really itchy and by 4pm that day, I was covered.

When I was questioned in Laganside Court about the devil and his existence and where he lives, the judge jokingly asked me if

I was looking towards the prosecution as I was answering. There were some light-hearted moments during the trial but the best part was that the people in court - the public gallery, lawyers and the judge had to listen to the entire service, singing and everything.

The whole sermon was played in the courtroom for forty-eight minutes, despite the controversial statement lasting only ten seconds. The court had to listen to the entire sermon in order to understand the context in which it was made. The main section they were interested in was as follows...

"I know the time will come in this land, in this land, Protestant Ulster, so-called Protestant Ulster, so-called evangelical Ulster, even Billy Graham said that Northern Ireland was the last bastion of the Gospel ... but ... I know the time will come in this land and in this nation, to say such things will be an offence to the law. It would be reckoned erroneous, unpatriotic. But I am in good company. The company of Luther and Knox and Calvin and Tindale and Lattimer and Cramner and Wesley and Spurgeon and such like."

"The Muslim religion was created many hundreds of years after Christ. Mohammed the Islam prophet was born around the year AD 570 but Muslims believe that Islam is the true religion dating back to Adam and that the biblical patriarchs were all Muslims including Noah and Abraham and Moses and even our Lord Jesus Christ."

"Today we see powerful evidence that more and more of Muslims are putting the Q'uran hatred of Christians and Jews alike into practice. Now people say there are good Muslims in Britain — that may be so — but I don't trust them. Enoch Powell was right and he lost his career because of it. Enoch Powell was a prophet and he told us that blood would flow in the streets and it has happened."

"Fifteen years ago Britain was concerned of IRA cells. Right throughout the nation they done a deal with the IRA because they were frightened of being bombed. Today a new evil has arisen — there are cells of Muslims right throughout Britain — can I hear an amen?"

"Right throughout Britain and this nation is going to enter into a great tribulation and a great trial. To judge by some of what I have heard in the past few months, you would think that Islam was little more than a variation of Christianity and Judaism. Not so. Islam's ideas about God, about humanity, about salvation are vastly different from the teaching of the Holy Scriptures. Islam is heathen, Islam is satanic, Islam is a doctrine spawned in hell."

What an amazing experience that was, bringing the Gospel into the court! I don't think anyone was converted but I was so pleased they got to hear it all. For all I know, that is possibly the first time some of them ever heard the Gospel.

The judge spent an hour summarising the case, and I was apprehensive at first because I heard a couple of the pastors beside me saying the verdict might go against me. We took a break for lunch and the general mood was not good. But in my heart, I felt God giving me peace.

Then the words were delivered - the judge said twice: "I find him not guilty."

District Judge Liam McNally said that while he considered the remarks to be offensive, he did not consider them grossly offensive under the law.

His exact words were: "The courts need to be very careful not to criticise speech, which however contemptible, is no more than offensive. It is not the task of the criminal law to censor offensive utterances. Accordingly, I find Pastor McConnell not guilty of both charges."

Applause rang out around Belfast Magistrates Court as the verdict was delivered and I shook hands with my defence lawyers.

I walked free from court after being acquitted of both charges.

We left the court and outside there were crowds of journalists waiting on me.

A large crowd sang hymns and cheered. I said: "Justice has been done!"

Afterwards we went out for a meal and I ordered stew, but couldn't eat it as I was too excited. I felt this experience was part of my ministry. This is what it should be. There are hundreds of preachers in the *comfort zone*. They aren't fighting the devil - they are fighting men.

Our government in Northern Ireland has failed in their responsibility to protect the very standard the country was founded on, which is freedom. We are now told what to say, how to say it, what to do, to the point of how to do it. If we don't do it, it is classed as hatred. The courts never saved me. They never stood up for me. In fact, if truth be told they failed and will fail you, as freedom is being dismantled all around us and we the church are sound asleep.

Are we seriously so blinded that we cannot see? Our right of freedom to say 'no' has been taken away from us. Yet are you aware once you take away *choice* you take away *freedom*? Scripture says; *'Choose you this day whom ye will serve?'* Joshua 24:15.

If we were created as robots we would never have been given *choice* by God. Listen carefully, God never created robots, that was man. God created the human soul and He teaches us through His Word how to make good choices for the purpose of our soul. We must change our ways, as it is written; *'Except a man be born again, he cannot see the kingdom of God.'* John 3:3.

As the end of the world closes in, God is going to release the 'body of Christ' into boldness. There will be a moving of the Spirit and thousands will be saved at any one time. In fact, as I write this book I have just heard over 3,000 souls were saved in Pakistan at the weekend – can I hear an Amen?

The Bible says in Matthew 16:18; *'The gates of hell shall not prevail against it!'* (the church). My friend, the gates in the Bible days was where they issued instructions on who was allowed into the city. The elders made the decision whether or not to allow someone in. The governments of this world are like those elders. They make decisions on the lives of the believer, but how do they understand 'spiritual things' if they are not led by the Spirit? Those decisions that they make will determine your future. They will tell you what to say and how to say it and if you don't…well, look out, persecution is coming but they will call it freedom!

But there is a King who wants to swing wide the door of Heaven for each one of us, yes, it all happened at Calvary. He seeks to bring you into His chamber of love, to cause you to abide under the shadow of His wings. And it will be in that place that your heart will sing in freedom, for it is where His love will melt away the fear within any of our souls.

Reflecting on the trial...

Since the trial God, in His Grace, has lovingly vindicated me, (as nearly every day in the United States, Europe and in the United Kingdom) Islamic fanatics have sought to destroy lives and upset our way of life! I feel it is dreadful what is happening in the world with persecution against the church and unless the government in this country wakens up and wises up, the same thing could happen on a larger scale! What happened to me was 'wee buns' but what is happening out in Europe, and other countries is just tragic.

I am not against any individual muslim. I would help them the best I could in any way possible. Things have got so bad, just as Jesus said it would. Jesus said; "Persecution would come." He said; "If the world hated me, they will hate you!" Islam is the world.

In Revelation 2:10, the Lord Jesus told the church at Smyrna; *'Fear none of those things which thou shalt suffer: behold, the devil shall cast some of you into prison, that ye may be tried; and ye shall have tribulation ten days: be thou faithful unto death, and I will give thee a crown of life.'*

Well we know outwardly, it wasn't satan, it was the police state of Smyrna at that particular time, but they were inspired by satan. I believe that this was satan wanting to put me in prison and testing me. When satan knew I was willing to go inside, it took the *pith* out of it. God answered prayer, He delivered me. In fact, the world heard my whole sermon, so the devil's plan was foiled as he ended up being my advertising board!

God can use trials to shape our characters.

I think God was testing me as I had been preaching for years. Did I believe in what I was saying? Did I believe in what I was preaching? Did I believe in who I was praying to? During this trial I stood on Hebrews 11:6; *'But without faith it is impossible to please him: for he that cometh to God must believe that he is, and that he is a rewarder of them that diligently seek him.'* I prayed this everyday, I told God: "I believe you are there."

My advice to anyone who is going through trials is this - stand on the Word of God! So many preachers are in the *comfort zone* today and I believe you will never be anything until you meet a giant in your life. Young David would still have been in the sheepfold with his father's sheep and would have done that his whole life if he hadn't met his giant. When Goliath came, David became a man. David won his spurs. A lot of preachers haven't won theirs.

David took five stones; why five? He took five because Goliath had four brothers and David was capable of taking them all out. Those five smooth stones were in the purpose of God, they were probably boulders for millenniums of time until the waters flowed over them, because he found the stones in the brook, in the water.

My Islam giant just suddenly appeared out of the blue, at least Israel heard Goliath for forty days. David only heard him for one day though, he went down on the 39th day and took him on. He knew five stones would do it, if Goliath and his family turned up! Only this time for me the giant wasn't a man, it was a system and the government sympathised with the system which proves they are away from God.

Saul put his armour on him but when David was set to go he was weighed down. He said; "I cannot go with these as I have not proved them." So what had he proved? He proved the anointing of God on him by Samuel and he proved the slingshot and his weapons.

2 Corinthians 10:4; *'For the weapons of our warfare are not carnal, but mighty through God to the pulling down of strong holds.'*

The Word of God was my stone to slay this giant in my life. Over the years I have a lot of stones saved up and I am ready to face my next giant!

Chapter Nineteen

LOVED BY GOD

When you study David there are not many people who do not like him because of the various likeable traits he had. He was Israel's sweetest singer, her most brilliant warrior and her best-loved king. David's name is a pattern for fidelity and friendship, bravery and love. We see him now a shepherd, we see him again with his hand on his harp. Look again and you'll see him challenging a giant to mortal combat and further on you will see him searching out the crippled grandson of his arch foe in special tenderness.

Sometimes you can catch him strong, sometimes tragically weak. Sometimes all together admirable and other times quite detestable but at all times, interesting. Even in his fall there is a splendour clinging to him.

The great truth is and no one can deny it – God loves this man. Isn't that amazing! God loves this man. He is a special chosen vessel of the Lord. He was of the elect, predestined, he was a factor in God's plan.

Call up his mistakes. Call up his faults. Call up his sins. Call up everything you can find and God will say to you when you have presented your argument: "I know, but I love him!" Let me say this again, present what you can to God but God will say: "I know, but I love him!"

Even you, the redeemed by the precious blood of the Lord Jesus and pardoned by His grace, your life can be full of dark patches, holes, sins and evils. Many of us have huge skeletons in the cupboard and yet Christ still loves us. Oh the grace of God is a wonderful thing.

Is it any wonder that Paul says in Romans 8:33; *'Who shall lay any thing to the charge of God's elect? It is God that justifieth.'*

I remember meeting a man who took great exception because God called David *'after mine own heart.'* (Acts 13:22) He then proceeded with great accuracy to tell me how bad David was, as if I didn't know. After he had finished he said: "Well what have you to say McConnell?" I replied: "Well, for my part there is no need to say anything. The last service God needs from me or you is the vindication of His character regarding His ways with men. God is God and He can do what He likes and He knows what He is doing!"

Do you know that God needs defending as much as the great Alps? I personally might not admire the greatness of the Alps or how much space they take up in Europe but who am I to question why they are there? Does it really matter? At no time do I need to be called upon to defend them. So, when Scripture describes one man as a man after God's own heart, I let that statement stand.

God has a clear right to pick His friends. No matter what you or I think. God made a covenant with David and God had no thought of breaking His covenant, even though He was aware of David's weaknesses and sins. But God knew that shepherd boy, that warrior, that king and God loved him.

I wish some pastors would rest in the calling of David, for they are struggling seeking to hold God's promise together and I know personally what that experience is like. Your sphere could be a humble and conspicuous flock where God has called you to minister, or perhaps a small gathering, but faithfulness to your task is always required of you. They might be an Eliab ready to tout you and speak contemptuously to you regarding those few sheep you are looking after out in a wilderness, not known, not recognised but this is what happened to young David.

David only came down to the battle where Goliath was, to deliver bread and cheese for his brothers. When David was shocked that there was no man who would take on Goliath, a guilty and a shamed Eliab smeared at him. "Away back to those sheep you were looking after in the wilderness!" Yet what had God noticed? – David's heart!

I want you to note… God notices! God notices when we are faithful in the little things such as looking after his father's sheep and running his father's messages with bread and cheese and God knew, if David loved that little flock that depended on him in the wilderness, then one day when He enlarged his capacity then he would love an entire nation that would depend on him.

Keep faithful in the little things and God will help you to be faithful in the big things, for this is what God can do for you...

'He chose David also his servant, and took him from the sheepfold's: from following the ewes great with young he brought him to feed Jacob his people, and Israel his inheritance. So he fed them according to the integrity of his heart; and guided them by the skilfulness of his hands.' Psalms 78:70-72.

God brings an unsophisticated shepherd boy into the palace for training by allowing Saul to introduce him to the court, to let him see and feel what court life would be like. To also let him see the power and politics that operated there. To let him hear matters of state and intrigue. Also the gossip and slander that went on in those high places. God brought His young servant into the court to hear all these things, and this was part of his training.

Another day would come when he would leave those few sheep and carry bread and cheese to his brothers on the front-line, a day that would change his life forever.

What is God doing with you? Is He secretly promoting you? Is He secretly dealing with you? I know what those experiences are like when God is moulding you and making you, turning you around, educating you, those are wonderful days, those are powerful days, those are mighty days. I remember as a young boy going through those seasons, some of which I have shared with you throughout this book.

This is the sort of God we are serving. A God who knows the end from the beginning, the God who created the end and created the beginning. He's a God we can trust and He is a God who is faithful to all of His children.

Samuel made a mistake by judging the outward appearance. Have you done the same? We need to learn that Samuel was not choosing but only registering God's choice. And the qualifications for God's king are inward not outward.

Take note, true greatness is the greatness of the Spirit.

David just didn't arrive on the front-line to fight Goliath without experience. Before Goliath was ever fought, David had won victories over the lion and the bear in the years before - Goliath was only another stepping stone. The question is, have you many victories?

This story teaches us that each victory is a step towards another giant. It teaches us if we have been careless in the lesser combats we will fail in the larger. If you cannot overcome the lesser battle do not expect to overcome the bigger battle. If I come wearing the garments that were won in the shade, I will win the big battle in the light of the blazing sun.

This is how we can be deceived! When we fail in something trivial we shrug our shoulders and say, 'ah nothing to worry about, when the big temptations come along I'll win them.' Listen carefully, that sort of reasoning is a fallacy, you're beat before you start! We have no guarantee of victory in the bigger things if we have not experienced victory in the smaller things. And this is a Scripture you need to take to heart; *'For who hath despised the day of small things?'* Zechariah 4:10. Never despise the day of small beginnings. As we used to sing in the Iron Hall; 'Each victory will help you some other to win.'

If you can get small answers to prayer, that's a sure sign that some day you're going to get big answers.

The reason David could face this monstrosity with such confidence was because in the secret place, he had proved the Lord in small things. Have you proved the Lord in small things? Have you proved the Lord in what the world would call insignificant things? David proved the Lord in small things!

Let's just look for a moment at David's little trophies hidden in his spiritual cupboard before he removed Goliath's head...

First trophy... It was memory of past help, that made him strong!

Our memories can do much to make us or mar us. They can make cowards or heroes of us all. It was past memories that made David strong. If I have acted unworthily a score of times, then what type of dead weight is that memory of failure? Or will I arise and be who I am meant to be, in the battle that sits before me? The Lord had delivered him from the lion and the bear. And David had dwelt on those deliverances, herding his sheep on those lonely hills so that his trust in God had grown into a fervent passion.

Think carefully, have you ever had answers to those little prayers? Have you ever had a deliverance you could share, even a small one? Had God come to you when you needed Him? The power that freed him from the lion's and bear's paws would never fail him when he would face the giant Goliath. David and God were alone on those hills, but a day would soon come when God and David would stand on a greater battlefield. God was with him on the mountains and God was not going to desert David in the valley. The God of your mountain-top experience is also the God in the valley. It's not what you are going through, it is where you are going to, that we need to remember!

Some of you may be facing a Goliath now while for others, your Goliath awaits. However, you do know, the bigger they are, the easier they are to hit and not miss them! Memories of your past victories in God is one trophy we all as Christians should have in our cupboard.

Second trophy… Proven realities!

David's experience of God was not second-hand. What are your experiences like? He didn't believe in God just because someone asked him to, he discovered God for himself. He was very conscious about his God in the hills of Judea as well as when he would have been in the tabernacle, the meeting place for God's people. And this is God's way, He teaches in secret that soul that He has elected to serve Him in public. The trouble with many so-called Christians and I love every one of you – your experience is second-hand, it's not real. There's a flaw in it, you must experience the reality of God.

Did you notice how David won his victory with the most unlikely of weapons? He had taken the helmet and sword of King Saul. The men of Israel might have thought he had some hope, but when they looked on David, still in his shepherd's garment, they shook their head in disbelief. But that is what people do when they meet a man or woman of experience in God – they look on in mock dismay. Don't you worry about the world or what they say; better still, don't worry about the so-called Christians who will seek to put you down like David's brothers who were in King Saul's army, a second-hand representation of God. Dear friend, keep your experiences in God. Better a well-used sling than an ill-used sword.

Never despise your little experiences with God. David had proved the staff, the sling-shot. I remember a servant of God saying to me years ago: "Jim McConnell, God has an anointing, but He has to find someone to anoint." And I am throwing this out to you now,

God has an anointing but He is looking for someone to anoint. And God found David, tell me, has He found you?

This is why God declares in Psalms 89:20; *'I have found David my servant!'* You would think God was sifting among humanity – "I am looking for somebody and I found David, my servant with my holy oil, I have anointed him."

David knew with his previous experiences there was no armour like God's armour. God was above him, God was beneath Him, God was on his right and left-hand side. David's God is my God, is He your God? I have trusted and served Him all these years and I can tell you, He has never let me down. But I have let Him down. You know what is wrong with us all? We do not trust God enough! We forget the promises of the Lord, Psalms 37:4; *'Delight thyself also in the LORD; and he shall give thee the desires of thine heart.'* We forget, Psalms 37:5; *'Commit thy way unto the LORD; trust also in him; and he shall bring it to pass.'* Proverbs 3:5, tells us; *'Trust in the LORD with all thine heart; and lean not unto thine own understanding.'* That's what it's all about.

'Then said David to the Philistine, Thou comest to me with a sword, and with a spear, and with a shield: but I come to thee in the name of the Lord of hosts, the God of the armies of Israel, whom thou hast defied. This day will the Lord deliver thee into mine hand; and I will smite thee, and take thine head from thee; and I will give the carcases of the host of the Philistines this day unto the fowls of the air, and to the wild beasts of the earth; that all the earth may know that there is a God in Israel. And all this assembly shall know that the Lord saveth not with sword and spear: for the battle is the Lord's, and he will give you into our hands.' 1 Samuel 17:45-47.

What a reality, David saw Him who is invisible (Colossians 1:15).

Listen to this old boy, you cannot enter ministry, you cannot kill the Goliaths, you cannot be all who you can be in God without the anointing that David carried. You need to get it! Are you asking

'How do I get it?' The answer is - walk the roads, fast, cry onto the Lord, stop debating, stop criticising, and He will fill you with Himself.

The country we live in needs anointed men and women and it's in that anointing you will be able to take your stand for Jesus no matter what type of Goliath stands in front of you. Whether sent from our UK government to whatever government you sit under, recognise there is a government higher than all – He's called Jesus!

I said it many years ago, I'll say it again, the Christian church here in Northern Ireland, UK, Europe etc is going to be persecuted while we yet sleep at the helm. If we are going to be who we are called to be, then we must become like David. Start stepping out, start winning small victories over your life, start recognising each one is a stepping stone into a greater awareness of who God really is. My friend, do you see God or the Goliath in front of you? Do you recall God's promises, His victories or do you hear the echo in the valley of your enemy? Allow God's reality to be louder in your walk than the noise of the enemy. And for this to happen you need the anointing that David carried.

Would you pray David's prayer, the one that melted his heart, the one that cried out to God, the one that realised you cannot be in God and Him not be real? As you pray David's prayer, don't be fearful, He is a God of love. Allow God to come and cleanse you, change you from the inside out, let's pray...

'Have mercy upon me, O God, according to thy lovingkindness: according unto the multitude of thy tender mercies blot out my transgressions. Wash me throughly from mine iniquity, and cleanse me from my sin. For I acknowledge my transgressions: and my sin is ever before me. Against thee, thee only, have I sinned, and done this evil in thy sight: that thou mightest be justified when thou speakest, and be clear when thou judgest. Behold, I was shapen in iniquity; and in sin did my mother conceive me. Behold, thou desirest truth in the inward parts: and in the hidden part thou shalt make me to know wisdom. Purge me with hyssop, and I shall be clean: wash me,

and I shall be whiter than snow. Make me to hear joy and gladness; that the bones which thou hast broken may rejoice. Hide thy face from my sins, and blot out all mine iniquities. Create in me a clean heart, O God; and renew a right spirit within me. Cast me not away from thy presence; and take not thy holy spirit from me. Restore unto me the joy of thy salvation; and uphold me with thy free spirit. Then will I teach transgressors thy ways; and sinners shall be converted unto thee. Deliver me from bloodguiltiness, O God, thou God of my salvation: and my tongue shall sing aloud of thy righteousness. O Lord, open thou my lips; and my mouth shall shew forth thy praise. For thou desirest not sacrifice; else would I give it: thou delightest not in burnt offering. The sacrifices of God are a broken spirit: a broken and a contrite heart, O God, thou wilt not despise.' Psalms 51:1-17.

Chapter Twenty

WHEN THE HOUSE DIVIDES

The Islam court case and the challenges which came with it certainly wasn't the worst trial in my lifetime. Throughout the court case, I slept every night, it never worried me one inch. I was willing to go to jail and I would have slept there quite happily as long as I got taking my Matthew Henry and a few other books with me. But a few years before that happened, my beloved Whitewell had a split. As I loved the church so much, it literally broke my heart. Whitewell at this point had been a move of God for fifty-two years. After this time it became simply a church and then the problems developed. I shed tears over it, had sleepless nights and I walked the roads because of the hurt that I experienced.

It gives me no pleasure to write about the split (if it could be avoided I would gladly let it go by) but this book is about – "*The Good, The Bad and Jesus Christ!*" My publisher said to me: "You must write about the hurts, the disappointments and the weaknesses of your life – as well as the successes! All of this contributes to the making of the man God wants you to be!"

I remember, it was a Sunday morning in June 2009 and our morning service was drawing to a close. I had just shared the Word of God and we were standing singing; 'Jesus how lovely you are.' I was standing on the stage, eyes closed, worshipping the Lord. As we reached the last line of the chorus, I opened my eyes and realised there was some commotion going on. I was shocked when I realised what was happening. I could see a number of the congregation had started walking out of the sanctuary.

In the corner of my eye, I caught a glimpse of some of the choir members taking their robes off and throwing them down, they too began to walk out. I was so disappointed but carried on; I pronounced the benediction and closed the service. I realised then, that the split that God had previously warned me about, was now happening!

There are many ways I could write this chapter about the good and the bad, but I want you to come to realise above all else, with what goes on in the world and even the church, we must focus on Jesus, as without Him, I likely wouldn't have made it through. He alone is worthy of all praise and honour. This happened to me when I was nearly 73 years old. When it was all over, I realised even then, when you are an old man God will test you.

I could go into the details of all that took place, what was said and what was done but I believe God is a restorer more than a divider. He's the God that loves His people more than He condemns them and He seeks only the best for His children. Our decisions should be made in reflection of who God is to us.

I write this Chapter with a heavy heart with those in mind; I seek only the best for everyone and that includes those who walked out that Sunday morning.

Three years before the split took place, God gave me a dream warning me that it was going to happen. Can I ask, 'Do you believe in dreams?' I shared earlier through my first encounter how we cannot believe in God and not believe in the supernatural.

One of the ways God communicates with His people, is through dreams. One of the most well known dreams in the Bible is where Joseph had a dream (Genesis 37) regarding his brothers and what was going to take place in his life. Who gave him the dream? God.

There's a man in the Bible who had a major fear issue called Gideon. How do I know he had fear? The Bible tells us (Judges 6) they had made dens in the mountain to hide from the Midianites, Amalekites and the children of the East. Who gave him the dream? God.

A dream from God will help break fear!

Then there is the story of Mary and Joseph, a story which is very well-known. We have all read the story but did you know Joseph not only was given one dream but the Bible tells us he had two. The first dream encouraged Joseph to take Mary as his wife (Matthew 1:20,21) and the second dream warned them (Matthew 2:13) to escape to Egypt. Can I ask again, who gave him the dream? The answer is God.

A dream from God will give you direction.

That same God that Joseph, Gideon, Daniel and many others received dreams from can be the same God that can direct you in the coming days in your life... if you would believe in the supernatural God!

The good news is, God still warns His people in dreams and a little over three years before the split, God had given me a dream that it was going to take place.

Knowing it was a God-given dream and a warning, I spoke to the people at a Friday night prayer meeting. I told them there was going to be a split and even though the dream showed me some of the people who would walk out, it is not God's will to expose, therefore I declined to say who it was.

I spoke openly about my thoughts regarding the split. The people were troubled, they asked me what to do, I told them to pray that the Lord would protect the work but warned them that it was going to happen.

As much as God warns His people and you seek to prepare yourself, nothing is ever as real as the time when it actually happens. Many of you reading this book may not be able to relate to a church split and the pain it causes but it is like a death.

We get the call (the dream) that those whom we love dearly are being taken out of our life and we have no control over it. The specialist (God) gives the news and you know it's only a matter of time; is it a day, week or year? Just over three years had passed for me.

While many saw the crowd walking out that morning, to me it was like sitting at a deathbed of a loved one in their home or hospital waiting for that time when life changes. Things are never quite the same, the seat you knew they always sat at, is now going to be empty. I was deeply saddened.

Following the walkout that Sunday, I went home with Margaret and we had our lunch. Later that day I spoke to some of my pastors; they were annoyed and I was annoyed.

If I said that I wasn't tempted to sit at the table of hatred, anger and resentment, that would be a lie. But I love that in the Scriptures, it mentions a place in I Corinthians called 'the judgement seat of Christ' where we will be called to give an account of our stewardship, our faithfulness, our attitudes, our agendas and our motives.

I was, despite my pain determined to carry on regardless. I went to the evening service and preached that night. I had to show myself as being strong for the people. The split never hindered us from winning souls or we didn't sit back and lick our sores. That following week we launched more prayer meetings and the church continued to grow again. Strife and tales were removed and souls were getting saved and honestly, souls are what matters!

I know at that time there were rumours and newspaper reports based on hearsay but as I am writing this book let me say this in all sincerity from my heart to those who walked out that Sunday morning. You have not been forgotten. An empty place remains in my heart for you. As Abraham Lincoln was asked; "If the southerners come back, what will you do? He said: "I will treat them as if they never left!"

To any pastor or people who have ever suffered in a split, let me say this… GOD IS BIGGER! Scripture states in Romans 11:29; '*For the gifts and calling of God are without repentance.*'

Sometimes the bread has to be broken to allow you to see what is really inside of it. Paul said; '*Be ye followers of me, even as I also am of Christ.*' 1 Corinthians 11:1

I may be just that wee boy all those years ago, who was raised up learning the ways of God and in some instances, we learn them by going through circumstance. I pray if anything, this chapter will help heal those of you who have endured the pain and suffering of a split.

When a thing like that happens to you, the devil expects you to go to a safe place where nobody knows you to nurse your wounds. Even though my heart was broken and the hurt was so severe, I picked myself up as there was no way I was going to let it destroy us. So like Gideon and his 300 chased the Midianites, I decided to fight the enemy of our souls. As Judges 8:4 says; '*faint, yet pursuing...*'

The Whitewell people opened up their homes all around the province and I went and ministered to whoever was there, preaching the Gospel. Each visit saw people being saved. We then started to give out leaflets advertising the rally at Ravenhill Rugby grounds, where 12,000 people turned out. It was a supernatural night and key conversions took place.

We refused to sit down and mope. We continued to knock on doors and we again booked the Odyssey in Belfast (picture on back cover) and 7,000 people turned out despite the heatwave and many souls were saved.

What could we do next? We rented the Shankill Leisure Centre in the Protestant community and it was packed to full capacity. Souls were being saved wherever we went, Whitewell was ticking again.

I am writing this to show you it is satan who is the defeated foe, not you! Christ defeated him at Calvary. Refuse to sit down and nurse your wounds. There is work to be done so let's get on with it. Friend don't allow fear to dominate you – fight it! Tramp on it! Call on the Name of Jesus, plead the Blood that was shed for you at Calvary and you will be the victor.

You and I will never know our potential under God. Not until we step out and take risks on the frontline of the battle!

My failing health...

Previous to the church split I had developed quinsy, a serious infection in my throat involving the development of abscesses.

I remember it well. It was a Mother's Day and I had preached that Sunday morning in agony.

We came home from church and I said to Linda: "Love, I am really ill here - would you deliver your testimony for me tonight?"

Linda said: "No, Daddy, no way. I'm not that type of person. I couldn't do that."

I told her: "Look, it's Mother's Day - do this for me as I'm ill."

So that night, Linda stood up and gave her testimony. I did an appeal at the end and I think five people responded that night. The next morning Linda took me to the hospital and the doctors actually had to lance my throat. I was kept in for a few days as they were afraid of the poison leaking and causing complications.

But it would have seemed the split had taken its toll on me; it was a whirlwind of a time. Dealing with the aftermath there was major deterioration in health. As a result the pastors in Whitewell started to get concerned. They wanted to know what they were going to do if something should happen to me. But they shouldn't have worried because as it is in the Bible, 'The successor never took over until the man in charge died.' However, we agreed that it was time to find someone that I could pass the baton to.

Chapter Twenty One

PASSING THE BATON

I am not sure if you are ready to read this or not, or even if you can handle it. But God thinks way past you and me. The sadness is, we cannot accept this, because so much spiritual air gets blown into our heads in a lot of churches on a Sunday of how great we are, that we think there is no-one else out there that God cares more for than our self.

Remember what I shared with you about the mirror? When you look in the mirror, never ask yourself how big am I, the question is, how small am I? Preaching today has become self-focused rather than Christ-focused.

The God who came into my life as a boy poured out without holding back. He says in Acts 2:39; *'For the promise is unto you, and to your children, and to all that are afar off, even as many as the Lord our God shall call.'*

Did you read that? God starts with you but He does not want it to end there; He wants to reach your children and their children and so on!

Scripture says; *'A good man leaveth an inheritance to his children's children.'* Proverbs 13:22.

There is no greater inheritance anyone of us could leave our children and their children than the inheritance of the Lord. When we understand God wants to reach through our bloodline, the generations coming after each of us, we will realise the importance and value in allowing God to do it through us. Let me tell you a story to reflect this…

It was in 1965 as I stood with a young baby only a few weeks old in my arms, presenting the child before the Lord. The congregation gathered as witnesses with his mum and dad.

That young boy grew under his father's and mother's godly counsel and under the ministry of the pastors of Whitewell and myself, attending church every week and at the age of thirteen, after one of my sermons he trusted Christ as his Lord and Saviour – that young man was David Purse.

He was 'called' to prepare for the Christian ministry through a prophetic utterance that I gave over him publicly at a church service when he was fifteen. From then on I took time to share with him about reading, preaching and serving the Lord.

I then watched him grow in his walk with the Lord and I took great joy in marrying him to his wife Donna. Later, I had the privilege of presenting their three sons to the Lord.

We were on a journey and in any journey through life, there is '*The good, The bad and Jesus Christ*' for those who serve Him.

A very painful moment for him and his family was when his father aged only 44, was murdered by terrorists in Belfast on 12th January 1980. He was David's father and my friend. I had the unenviable task of breaking the news to him. I remember going to find him in his house and he was drying his hair to go to the youth meeting and I dried it for him. I told him what had happened to his dad. I still recall how we cried together holding each other that dark January evening.

David's father was one of the foundational members of

Whitewell, a good man; never to be forgotten, he gave the first ministry in tongues in Whitewell. His dad's brother, Charlie, was one of the original ten and is still in attendance.

I chose David Purse as my successor because he had a key ingredient in his character – he trusted that God was God in all things. He was there for the will of God not for the will of David Purse, he would do whatever had to be done.

When I consulted the rest of our pastors, each one was in total agreement about David, he was the one.

Over the years he would have visited us at Whitewell, in many instances to minister at a Sunday service or Wednesday Bible study, other times we would chat privately – like a father and son. It was not a strange thing when I phoned him and asked if he could come to the church to see me.

When he arrived he joined the pastors and me and I put the question to him: "The pastors and I want to ask you if you would take over from me?"

You will never guess what he said… it showed the purity of heart, he said: "No!"

He said 'no' because he wanted something greater than the successor title of James McConnell, something greater than a multi-million-pound church, he wanted to be sure it was God!

Over a period of several months through prayer and seeking godly counsel from men who are not influenced by titles, numbers, money etc. David called me one day and said that he would accept. It confirmed the maturity he carried.

David had pastored a church in Withernsey, in Yorkshire, England for twenty years before returning to Northern Ireland and was pastoring in Cullybackey Elim before the move to be an associate pastor to Whitewell congregation. A position he served in for four years exactly before I handed the reins over to him on 1st September 2014.

During those four years we sat and had breakfast together every morning. I tried to teach him everything I knew. Pancakes and syrup mixed with good advice.

Some leaders when they get their position think they have made it, but in truth, one is only starting. Every morning at 7am he was at his office, a man who is a worker and not scared to dirty his hands.

Preaching twice a week, every Sunday morning and every Wednesday night. He was on three Sunday mornings a month, I preached one full Sunday a month, morning and evening.

Yet during those four years what I didn't realise was the church split had taken its toll on me. It quite literally broke my heart.

We were just getting David officially on-board and within the third month from him starting, I took a heart attack.

It was a Sunday morning and I was getting ready for church, I was just out of the shower and my legs went like rubber. I had no pain but just felt awful, the sweat was running off me. I shouted at Margaret and then Linda and David arrived. I told David, "Sorry, you will have to preach!"

The ambulance arrived and took me to hospital for emergency treatment. It was really frightening for the whole family because at one stage, I almost died.

They took me to Antrim Area Hospital and then they transferred me to the Royal Hospital in Belfast and they just said: "It's not too bad, we will give you stints." But when they had me opened up they said: "Send him back." I ended up having a quadruple bypass and a new valve fitted as my heart was badly damaged.

I had to wait three months before the bypass surgery was scheduled and then I had to recover so this gave David Purse time to get used to running the church. I was out of church about five months. I didn't like being in the hospital, I used to walk the corridors just pushing my drips with me.

Whitewell was my baby and it was hard to hand it over but I knew the time was right. Nothing happened without my permission; I was like the pope in Whitewell but my body was failing. I was no longer that young preacher that started out in Whitewell, time had called and I knew I couldn't keep going. I knew David was a good preacher but I also knew he would hold the people. I knew he would manage as he was capable of keeping the ship steady in the water. He is a hard worker, he does what I did. He comes in early every morning and runs the church well. He is not like many leaders out there that sit about scratching themselves.

On 1st September 2014, we had a huge induction service that Sunday night. All his family came, the place was packed out. I handed all over to him. I entered the church as Senior Pastor with the responsibility of several thousand people, when I would enter again, I would enter as a member with the responsibility for one – me!

If I am not there to preach, I sit with Tommy Kearns, one of the original ten at the back of the church. Sometimes you could catch us smiling like the two old men from the muppets.

I know some will ask, how can that be? From a pastor to a member? Listen, titles are just that – a title, fruit is what is important. I am still James McConnell, the one who was forged through the good and the bad by Jesus Christ.

The responsibility of running the church is removed, but the responsibility that I always carried before Whitewell remains the same today in my life – to love Jesus Christ.

As I sat to write this part I was reminded of an old photo of me walking towards the front entrance of the first church where we started our meetings all those years ago. Within that photo a young boy wearing shorts was following me. Do you know who it was? That little boy was David Purse. Was it prophetic or by chance? I know one thing, when God moves, He moves through generations. Raised in the house of the Lord and now pastoring that same house, as Scripture states; '*...as for me and my house, we will serve the Lord.*' Joshua 24:15. Dedicated to David Purse Senior

Chapter Twenty-two

TURNING FEAR TO FAITH

As an orphan boy running around, God taught me, through my training, not to be afraid. The promise is in the Word of God - actually there are 365 fear nots in the Bible, so there is one for each day. Back then, my main fear was insecurity and what was going to happen to me, because my grandparents were elderly and my sister was dying. I had nothing, and no one to turn to. However through the years, that fear manifested itself in other areas of my life.

Following my ill health from the church split, I took cancer. A couple of the girls from Whitewell worked in the Ulster Clinic so I went there for a check up and I saw Professor Keane, he was a right character! He examined me and then he sent for me, I remember going back to see him that night. I sat in his office and he said: "Sorry to tell you this pastor but you've got bloody cancer!"

And I said: "Right okay."
He said: "You are a man of God, you should be able to take it!"
I told him: "No problem, there are thousands like me."

I wasn't worried about it. I believe God is keeping me alive. Following the diagnosis, I had to undergo treatment, I had chemotherapy and radiotherapy. Part of my bowel was damaged due to the treatment. However during my treatment, I still continued to preach.

I was believing God for healing. For me it was just a nuisance, I wanted this illness over me so I could get back into the fray. Even retirement is a nuisance to me to be honest. I knew it was just fear trying to steal my joy so I wasn't going to give in. I was determined to ignore the workings of the devil. Don't you know, he is a liar. It is important that we do not listen to his words.

Known as the *Prince of Preacher's*, Charles Haddon Spurgeon, a Baptist preacher talks about; *'Letting it go in one ear and out the other.'* I'm conscious of this and have tried over the years to follow this recommendation. Mostly, I feel, I am successful but sometimes I can still feel a tune seek to whistle from my lips. My situation is like Martin Luther King Jr. said: "You cannot keep birds from flying over your head but you can keep them from building a nest in your hair."

The more you allow people to annoy you, the more you will lose your vision. One philosopher said, "if you want to destroy a man with a vision - give him another one."

The Scripture I would like to bring to your attention is the popular verse in Nehemiah 6:3; *'I am doing a great work, so that I cannot come down: why should the work cease, whilst I leave it, and come down to you?'*

What were Sanballat and Geshem seeking to do to Nehemiah? They wanted to give him another vision and they sought him to come to one of the villages in the plain of Ono and the answer from him was oh no!

You must remember the *'provision'* comes in the *'vision.'* I thank God that Whitewell was a bunch of workers. They worked through rain, hail and snow, battling the elements to build buildings, erect crusades, witness on the streets, travel to foreign lands, all because vision had captured them.

The anointing of God and the presence of God keeps me going. If I have that sense of God with me, then I am not afraid of anything. I think that fear makes a man act a certain way.

It's like the fear of cancer being worse than the cancer itself. I have got rid of that fear; I am not frightened. I think that is the secret of my strength as I am not afraid. I am not afraid of the devil, but I fear the Lord. I acknowledge Him, I am conscious of Him, I love Him, I desire Him.

If you are dealing with fear in your own life, remember that there is a fear-not in the Bible for every day of the year. The fear of death is worse than death itself. In Hebrews 2:15, it refers to fear of death is subject to bondage. Fear brings bondage.

If God speaks to you, it will line up with His Word and it will also have a supernatural element. It is like the night I experienced in Finaghy when the Spirit spoke to me about filling the King's Hall - this was the sword of the Lord and Gideon for all to see.

I have known that same voice since I was a boy. As the Scripture says: *'My sheep hear my voice, and I know them...'* John 10:27

I recall the story of an American who came to the highlands of Scotland. He was reading that Scripture.

He said to the shepherd: "Let me wear your clothes," and he walked among the sheep and he called them and they ignored them.

But the shepherd put on the American's clothes and he shouted and they came to him because it was the voice they knew.

A spirit of fear...

I have found, in my ministry and life-time, that many sincere, Godly people are affected by fear. They battle with it; they cannot overcome it for it dominates and what dominates – controls!

Paul, writing to Timothy, calls it '*a spirit.*' He says in 2 Timothy 1:7; *'For God hath not given us the spirit of fear; but of power, and of love, and of a sound mind.'*

It is important to know what God has given and what He has not given to you. Note again, Paul did not refer to the 'spirit' as the Holy Spirit but a spirit. That spirit does not belong to God. That spirit does not belong to Heaven. That spirit is evil. His method is to create it's character through us, to make us constantly feel insecure and useless, so that we will never be free to run the race that God has called us to without fear demanding you to bow to it.

Brothers and sisters - fear is the dark room where negatives are developed! That's why we are constantly urged in the Epistles to; "Walk in the light." So, I urge you to come out of that dark room in your mind! The enemy had kept Gideon in a cave (Judges 6) seeking to develop the negatives while all the time God was calling him out – hear His voice today – He is calling you out of that cave, walk into His glorious light, do not be afraid, He has not called us to fear but to faith in Him.

When you finish this book, I urge you to read the first three chapters of the Book of Job. Job is described as a perfect (or an upright) one that feared (or honoured) God and avoided evil. Yet Job had a weakness and that weakness was fear! That fear brought Job constant insecurity, even though he was the wealthiest man in the east.

Job's fear was a threefold fear. He feared poverty; he feared sickness and he feared for his family. Even when he worshipped God or prayed, he was afraid. When he heard his sons and daughters were feasting, he offered up burnt offerings to each of them. His reason was – "It may be that my sons have sinned and cursed God in their hearts." We are also told – "Thus did Job continually."

Fear dominated him and, when he had lost all – his wealth, his health and his sons and daughters he cried, *'For the thing which I greatly feared is come upon me and that which I was afraid of is come unto me. I was not in safety, neither had I rest, neither was I quiet; yet trouble came.'* Job 3:25-26

After this, God began to deal with Job until Job began to believe

God and have positive faith in Him. We are told in Job 42:12, 13, 15 '*So the Lord blessed the latter end of Job more than his beginning. For he had fourteen thousand sheep and six thousand camels and a thousand yoke of oxen and a thousand she-asses. He had also seven sons and three daughters. And in all the land were no women found so fair as the daughters of Job...*'

After this, Job lived one hundred and forty years and saw his son and his son's sons – he witnessed four generations. So Job died being old and full of days. That's what faith in God can do for you, brother and sister.

Fear is of the devil! Get rid of it by calling on the name of the Lord and you will experience what Isaiah said in Isaiah 26:3; '*Thou wilt keep him in perfect peace whose mind is stayed on thee.*' Note the word 'stayed' – there's the secret! Think about Jesus. Worship Jesus. Sing to Jesus. Pray to Jesus. Witness about Jesus. Love Jesus. Your fear will go!

Let me close this chapter concerning fear by telling you a story. Throughout my years in the ministry, I have encouraged and counselled believers who are afraid of death – maybe there is someone reading this book who is afraid of dying?

There was a vicar a hundred years ago who was dying. A fellow vicar came to see him and, as usual, he opened the Scriptures to read to him and comfort him. Suddenly the vicar who was dying said to his friend: "Read to me I Samuel 17."

His friend replied: "That's the story of David and Goliath?"
"I know," he replied. "Read it to me!"

His friend did so and he came to verse 45 where David said to the Philistine – '*Thou comest to me with a sword and with a spear and with a shield; but I come to thee in the name of the Lord of Hosts, the God of the armies of Israel whom thou hast defied!*' He was still surprised at such a reading on his death-bed.

When he had finished reading verse 45, the dying vicar cried out: "O death, you're coming to me with your dark valley and your cold, icy waters; but I come to thee in the name of the Lord of Hosts! The Lord Jesus Christ, the Captain of my salvation, who has taken the sting out of death and robbed the grave of its victory! Death, you are defeated by my Lord and now I triumph by the presence of Jesus!"

The psalmist David was right when he said; '*Yea, though I walk through the valley of the shadow of death, I will fear no evil, for thou art with me!*' Psalms 23:4

Fear is only a shadow of a thought. The question is what thought are you allowing to control you today? Paul tells the brethren, you (if you're born-again) and I what type of thought we should introduce into our lives…

'*Finally, brethren, whatsoever things are true, whatsoever things are honest, whatsoever things are just, whatsoever things are pure, whatsoever things are lovely, whatsoever things are of good report; if there be any virtue, and if there be any praise, think on these things.*' Philippians 4:8.

Chapter Twenty-three

THE ROYAL HEM

I want to close this book sharing with you, my dear friend, about the most important person in my whole life – Jesus Christ!

Whether you're a church goer or not, born-again Christian or Muslim, atheist or theist, one thing I know is sure – my story is *my* story and without Jesus I would not be who I am!

If you are ever going to be who you are called to be, one must learn to press through the crowd that stands around you and in fact on many occasions will separate you from your entitlement in God – Jesus Christ!

I have shared in the previous chapters…
Planting pots – Where the doctrine you accept can stop you from growing in God.
Controversial Mentors – Who you walk beside will determine the path you take.
13 Years lost – You must break man's red-tape to receive Christ's Blood bought freedom.

To be who you are in God you must press through what stands between you and Him.

There's a story in the Bible of a lady (Luke 8) who was sick and for many years she had been attending the doctors – even professionals were not able to help her.

A day came that she heard about Jesus. Did she wonder, could it be true what she heard about Him? Was He able to deliver her from the need she had? She decided to find out!

The lady set her fear aside of not being allowed to touch anyone, due to her illness and the Jewish Law. She pressed through the crowd that separated her and touched the royal hem of Jesus.

You must decide to do the same if you are to walk in the fullness that God has for you. Take a step against fear and like David, learn to run at the voice of the one who threatens you. Whether a disease, jail or fear of man – which is one of the biggest.

The sermons in churches today have been watered down to appease this generation, is it any wonder revival has been kept away? If we seek revival in our country, then we must ask why we have raised a generation of brats.

Paul writes; '*When I was a child, I spake as a child, I understood as a child, I thought as a child: but when I became a man, I put away childish things.*' 1 Corinthians 13:11

Something I detest is a spoilt brat! If you do not know what a spoilt brat is, basically I am referring to a child that has their parents wrapped around their little finger. The child squeals, roars, cries, jumps up and down, throws things, smashes things, lies on the floor all for one reason – to get what they want, not thinking about the parent.

This may waken you up as a Christian but we have spoilt Christian brats! Their prayer is give me, give me, give me. Church leaders have raised a generation of spoilt brats with 'self' being their altar of worship and we wonder why we do not have a move of God?

Your church or your wee group may have room for spoilt brats but the 'Kingdom of God' does not. If you really, really want God to be real in your life then realise the key;

'...If any man will come after me, let him deny himself, and take up his cross daily, and follow me.' Luke 9:23

The message of 'flesh-denial' has been removed from the churches and replaced with praying for more material things to adorn who? Self!

There is only One King in the kingdom, He is to be served, He is to be adored and to be loved – this was how I found that out...

In the mid-1960s, I was invited by a precious man of God, Pieter Quist, to preach at a youth rally in the city of Rotterdam. As I prepared to board the aircraft at Heathrow Airport, the announcer said that the flight would be delayed for a couple of hours because the plane had developed a technical fault. Those who travelled in those days will remember the vouchers distributed for beverages and sandwiches.

I found myself sitting beside this very dignified gentleman. He was immaculately dressed because he was on a business trip. He seemed so important whereas I felt so inferior. I was wearing a shiny suit, well, shiny because my wife Margaret had just pressed it one too many times! But it was all I had to impress.

Within a few minutes, the gentleman and I engaged in a conversation about various things to pass the time when the announcer relayed over the tannoy: "Refreshments are now ready to be served!" The two of us went together. He ordered whiskey and I asked for Coca Cola. Then, after a while, it was announced over the tannoy there were more drinks. He again ordered a whiskey. I asked for an orange drink. I was conscious of him watching me. Then, after another period of time, the announcement was delivered for more refreshments. He again went with me to the counter and ordered a gin and tonic. I had a lemonade.

Suddenly he asked me – "Who are you? What are you? What do you do?" He looked at me intently. I was about to tell him by putting on my best accent – "Sir I am a minister of the Gospel and I'm going to preach in Rotterdam!" Self was being adorned. However, the Holy Spirit stopped me in my tracks and whispered to me – "Tell him you love me!" You can imagine how fast my thoughts were shooting through my mind, and they were suggesting to me that I shouldn't say this.

Realising the Holy Spirit never gets it wrong I said: "Sir, I love the Lord Jesus Christ with all my heart and I have sought to serve Him from the age of eight!"

His eyes widened. I thought he was going to faint. He spluttered: "Young man, I have never heard anybody talk with such conviction like that in my whole life and furthermore, I have never met anyone like you in my life!"

He continued: "Why, you would think the person you are talking about is still alive! Are you for real?"

Before he finished saying 'real' I jumped in shouting: "He is alive! He died at Calvary and rose from the dead! He's changed my life. He looked after me when I was a boy. I cannot live without Him. I do love Him and He also loves you!"

We talked for some time and then the announcement came to board the plane. We shook hands and he was led to first class and I was led to economy. You might think, that's not nice… him first class and me economy? But let me say, he may enjoy first-class in this life but I know I will be travelling heavenly-class in the Spirit – Can I hear an amen?

You see, that day I could have hesitated, in fact I did, but even in our hesitation God gives grace for us to still step up and honour Him by NEVER being afraid to tell men and women that you love Him! It is important for you to witness and it's amazing the effect it has on those you tell it to. That's what John wrote in his epistle in 1 John 4:19; '*…we love him because he first loved us.*'

Salvation is not just a fire escape and I do believe in Hell and eternal punishment. Salvation is a lovely and personal relationship between you and your Living Lord.

Being orphaned as a youth and not being educated, I have talked with Him all my life (from the age of eight to nearly 80 now – that's a lot of talking!).

He's my Father and my Mother; my Sister and my Brother! He's everything to me! I say this with deep respect (and I have met many friends over the years) Jesus is more real to me than any of them!

He's my personal Saviour!
He's my Lord!
He has become a Friend, a Confidante, a Guide, and a Protector!
Once again, a thousand times I say, I love Him!

It's like the portion of Scripture in the Song of Solomon 2:16; *"My beloved is mine, and I am his!"* That's what I think of Jesus!

Lean a little closer, something else I want to tell you… let me whisper it… the Lord Jesus wants men and women to love Him – that's what I told the man at the airport.

Do you remember the scene at the Sea of Galilee recorded in John 21, when the Master revealed Himself to seven of His disciples and cooked breakfast for them, and I am sure it wasn't an Ulster Fry[1] (John emphasises this was the third time that Jesus showed Himself to the disciples - after that He was risen from the dead). Then in verse 15 (John records); 'So when they had dined... (Jesus waited until their bellies were full) Jesus saith to Simon Peter, Do you love me?' In fact, Jesus asked Peter that question three times – "Do you love Me?"

Here is the risen Saviour and Lord. The conqueror of death, hell and the grave; the creator of one hundred and fifty billion galaxies and all Jesus is concerned about was that a crude, rude, impetuous fisherman loved Him. This has to show us the heart of Jesus! He

1 Ulster Fry is fried bread and meat

loves and wants to be loved. He said to Peter three times – "Do you love Me?" Of course a few days before, Peter had denied Him three times. Jesus was calling Peter to repentance and with that comes restoration.

Yet, it was that very question Jesus put to Peter that gripped me! DO YOU LOVE ME?

Paul writes in 1 Corinthians 13;

'Though I speak with the tongues of men and of angels, but have not love, I have become sounding brass or a clanging cymbal. And though I have the gift of prophecy, and understand all mysteries and all knowledge, and though I have all faith, so that I could remove mountains, but have not love, I am nothing. And though I bestow all my goods to feed the poor, and though I give my body to be burned, but have not love, it profits me nothing.

Love suffers long and is kind; love does not envy; love does not parade itself, is not puffed up; does not behave rudely, does not seek its own, is not provoked, thinks no evil; does not rejoice in iniquity, but rejoices in the truth; bears all things, believes all things, hopes all things, endures all things.

Love never fails. But whether there are prophecies, they will fail; whether there are tongues, they will cease; whether there is knowledge, it will vanish away. For we know in part and we prophesy in part. But when that which is perfect has come, then that which is in part will be done away.

When I was a child, I spoke as a child, I understood as a child, I thought as a child; but when I became a man, I put away childish things. For now we see in a mirror, dimly, but then face to face. Now I know in part, but then I shall know just as I also am known.

And now abide faith, hope, love, these three; but the greatest of these is love.'

We would say, when Jesus asked the questions to Peter, "do

you love me?" This is a question you might put to a child! Yet the question was practical as well as gracious, because love is the true qualification of labour! A person cannot labour effectively for Christ if he does not love Christ. Man cannot go beyond his inspiration. What is the greatest factor in the Christian life? Love to Christ and love for Christ!

Because of love, forgiveness is interweaved with it. Scripture says; *'But God commandeth his love toward us, in that, while we were yet sinners, Christ died for us.'* Romans 5:8.

All those years ago, while James McConnell was sinning and thinking about sinning, Christ died for me! Can we take a moment to think about this? While you and I were sinning and thinking about sinning, failing, making mistakes, knowing we would maybe even run from Him, He left Heaven, dressed Himself in a bodysuit, walked those dusty paths of Calvary, and did not even fight with what was happening but as Scripture says, *'he laid down his life for us.'* 1 John 3:16. He is without doubt love manifested!

Listen to Jesus in John 14:23, this is beautiful. He says; *'If a man love me, he will keep my words and my Father will love him; and we will come unto him and make our abode with him!'*

This is my life or, better still, He is my life. Let Him come into your life – you will find, with Him, life is worth living! Even more wonderful – you will be living with Him for all eternity – and that is a long time!

After this, Peter was restored, recommissioned and equipped to do the work Jesus had planned for him to do. So much so, that He filled him with the Holy Ghost (in Acts 2) and used him to lead three thousand souls into the kingdom on the day of Pentecost.

Yet, do you know what was behind Peter's restoration and forgiveness? The private prayer life of Jesus! Listen to Jesus on the night of the Passover in Luke 22:31-32, He looks at Peter and says; *'Simon, Simon, behold satan hath desired to have you that he may sift you as wheat; but I have prayed for thee that thy faith fail not and, when thou art converted, strengthen thy brethren!'*

The same Jesus is praying for you and I. He's our Great High Priest, our Man in the Glory, our Mediator! Many of us have yet to discover the secret of our success – it is all because He is praying for us! Friend, it doesn't matter who is praying or who is not praying for you – just as long as He is praying for you!

There is one more thing I wish to say. Notice what Jesus said to Peter; "*....when thou art converted, strengthen thy brethren!*" In other words, Jesus was telling him - "Just as I have lifted you Peter, you now lift others! Just as I have forgiven you Peter, you forgive others by a loving and gentle spirit. Just as I have strengthened you, then you in turn will strengthen others!" It's like a repeat of what God said to Abraham in Genesis 12: *'I will bless thee... and thou shalt be a blessing.'*

Friend, let God have His way in your life. If you do, He may ask you to get right with that person; forgive that person and ask that person to forgive you, or give that person another chance as he has given you many chances! Many times we forget what He said in Matthew 6:12 *'And forgive us our debts as we forgive our debtors.'*

Just before we end, I would be honoured if you would let me pray this prayer with you.

Father,
I come to you in the Holy Name of Jesus. I thank you for sending your Son to die for me at Calvary and I thank you He was willing to come. Will you forgive me of all my sin?

Will you come into my heart and You, by truly coming into my heart, will change my life. Cleanse me and wash me in the blood that you shed for me at Calvary. I not only need You but I want You!

Now Father, will you guide and guard me for the rest of my life? Keep me faithful and let me grow in grace and in the knowledge of my Lord and Saviour, Jesus Christ. I ask this for Your honour and glory.

Amen.

If you have prayed this prayer or ***'The Good, The Bad & Jesus Christ'*** has helped you, please feel free to contact me at:

Pastor James McConnell
Whitewell Metropolitan Tabernacle
837 – 868 Shore Road
BELFAST
Northern Ireland
BT15 4HS
E. info@jamesmcconnell.org
W. www.JamesMcConnell.org

At 13 I had preached my first sermon and at 16 years of age I scripted the following, the original paper I still hold.

Who is Jesus? He is...

- **Jehovah Jireh** – The Lord that will provide
- **Jehovah Nissi** – The Lord our banner
- **Jehovah Rapha** – The Lord that healeth
- **Jehovah Shalom** – The Lord our peace
- **Jehovah Tsidkenu** – The Lord our righteousness
- **Jehovah Raah** – The Lord our shepherd
- **Jehovah Shammah** – The Lord is present
- **Jehovah Saboath** – The Lord of hosts
- Adam's creator
- Eve's promised seed
- Abel's testifier
- Enoch's companion
- Noah's true saving ark
- Abraham's El Shaddai
- Isaac's substitute
- Jacob's wrestler
- Joseph's shepherd and stone of Israel
- The One who brought the children out of Egypt
- The Rock from which they drank
- The Manna from that they did eat
- The pillar of cloud by day
- The pillar of fire by night
- Moses' prophet that should come
- Aaron's rod that budded
- Joshua's captain

- Rahab's scarlet cord
- Deborah's song
- Samson's strength
- Shamgar's goad
- Gideon's sword
- Samuel's strength of Israel who will not lie nor repent
- David's slingshot
- Solomon's wisdom
- David's mantle
- Elisha's double portion
- Nehemiah's joy
- Isaiah's righteous servant
- Jeremiah's righteous branch
- Ezekiel's man of fire
- Daniel's ancient of days
- Hosea's ever-faithful husband
- Joel's restorer of wasted years
- Micah's ruler whose going forth have been of old – from everlasting
- Haggai's desire of all nations
- Zechariah's Jehovah's fellow
- Malachi's sun of righteousness – with healing in His wings
- The One who shut the lions mouth
- The One who quenched the violence of fire
- The King that shall reign in righteousness
- The royal diadem of beauty
- The hope of Israel
- The fountain of living waters
- The hiding place and the covert from the tempest

- Rivers of water in a dry place
- The shadow of a great rock in a weary land
- The rose of Sharon
- The lily of the valley
- The bright and morning star
- The banner over me is love
- His head is as the most-fine gold, His locks are black and bushy
- He is white and ruddy – the chiefest amongst ten thousand
- His mouth is so sweet – yea He is altogether lovely
- His hands drop sweet smelling myrrh
- His garments smell of myrrh, aloes and cassia
- His presence brings joy
- At His right hand they are pleasures for evermore
- His name is as an ointment poured forth
- He's the lamb of God
- The Shepherd of the sheep
- The door of the fold
- The Bread of life
- The true vine
- The dayspring from on High.
- The light of the world
- The daystar in our hearts
- The angel of the covenant
- The Word of God
- The heart of God
- The love of God
- The arm of God

- The power of God
- The wisdom of God
- The brightness of His glory
- The image of the invisible God
- The fullness of the Godhead bodily
- The last Adam
- The Mediator of the new covenant
- The mediator between God and man
- The head of the body
- Lord of the churches
- God of the Church
- The stone that was set at nought of the builder's
- The chief corner stone
- The great apostle of our profession
- The great prophet the Lord raised up
- The great evangelist who came to save the lost
- The chief shepherd
- The bishop of our souls
- Our great elder brother
- The Rabbi – Teacher sent from God
- Matthew's Saviour
- Luke's son of man
- John's son of God
- Nathaniel's King of Israel
- Philip's 'Father'
- Thomas – Lord of me and the God of me
- Peter's rock
- Paul's potter who has power over the clay
- Jude's only wise God and our Saviour

- Hannah's prayer answerer
- Mary's God my Saviour
- Magdalene's 'Rabboni'
- Lydia's heart opener
- Ruth's goel – kinsman redeemer
- Prince and Saviour
- The great God and our Saviour
- The Eternal King
- The Invisible God
- The only wise God
- Only potentate who hath immortality
- The resurrection
- The life
- Eternal life
- The same yesterday, today and forever
- Firstborn
- First-begotten from the dead
- First fruits from them that sleep
- The first and the last (the beginning and the ending)
- The author
- The finisher of our faith
- The Alpha
- The Omega
- The Father to His divinity
- The Son as to His humanity
- The Holy Ghost in the hearts of people
- The lion of the tribe of Judah
- The root and the offspring of David
- The great I am

- Emmanuel – God with us
- Wonderful
- Counsellor
- Mighty God
- Everlasting Father
- Prince of peace
- King of kings
- Lord of lords

This is my beloved; this is my friend.